#Impress Yourself

By: Candace Thompson

Foreword by: Tamika L. Sims, Amazon Award-Winning and Bestselling Author, Author Coach & Editor

Limits of Liability and Disclaimer of Warranty

The author and publisher shall not be liable for your misuse of this material. This book is strictly for informational and educational purposes.

Warning – Disclaimer

The purpose of this book is to educate and entertain. The author and/or publisher do not guarantee that anyone following these techniques, suggestions, tips, ideas, or strategies will become successful. The author and/or publisher shall have neither liability nor responsibility to anyone with respect to any loss or damage caused, or alleged to be caused, directly or indirectly by the information shared in this book.

All graphic images used within this text have been created solely for the purpose of this book and created explicitly by the author.

Cover art is original art created by Canvases With Candace LLC.

ISBN: 978-0-578-56237-7

Dedication

Dedicated to who I *used* to be.

Acknowledgements

First, I must thank God because without the talent and gifts You have blessed me with, none of this would be possible.

Thank you to my parents Michael and Lydia; for ALWAYS believing in me and encouraging me to be my authentic self. Teaching me to love myself has been one of the most valuable lessons I have learned, specifically because of the way you love me.

To my sister LaDawna, thank you for consistently being my guinea pig and inspiration even when you didn't realize it.

To my circle and tribe, without you ALL; our late-night lengthy talks, your ear to listen, shoulders to lean on, and your belief and encouragement in some of my darkest days, I'm not sure where I would be.

Because these people have been impressed with me from day one, I have finally been able to impress myself.

Foreword

It is hard to believe that I only met Candace May 25, 2019. From that Saturday morning, until now, she has kept a high, consistent energy that has been unmatched from other client experiences. I've worked with more than 100 authors, and she is truly in a class by herself. She never once lost momentum and submitted herself to the entire creative process, no matter how much I stretched and challenged her. For it not to be even 90 days later, at the time of publishing, to be holding this manuscript in my hands, is nothing short of amazing. I applaud and honor her.

The premise behind *Impress Yourself* is confidence, security and validation - in you. For far too long, we have allowed society to define us - to tell us who we are and to tell us whether we are too fat, or too thin. Too tall or too short. Too smart or too dumb. Too successful or not. We have allowed society to creep into every crevice of our minds and our lives because we have not yet realized the power of our voices.

We have become silenced. We have shrunken under the light of others and we have become unimpressed even with ourselves. This is why a book such as *Impress Yourself* is so important because it helps to change our language and our mindset, which are both very important to our personal growth and development.

Author Candace Thompson has done an amazing job providing a combination of anecdotal stories, practical lessons and hands-on exercises and activities to help you become impressed with the person, that at the end of the day matters the most - you.

I am beaming with pride at the work that Candace has done. She has been a stellar student, even breaking my personal coaching record, and no matter what, I will always be impressed with that.

But, don't take my word for it. Allow Candace's hard work to speak for itself.

Tamika L. Sims,

Chief Creative

Get Write With Tamika

Amazon Bestselling & Award-winning Author | Author Coach | Editor

Note from the Author...

Hey Friend! I am so excited to take this journey with you. Ok, so if you are anything like me, you probably have a notebook with you to jot down notes and thoughts. Aht Aht, put it down! This is *your* book. This maybe a little uncomfortable, but grab your favorite pen, highlighter and let's get to work. I want you to write directly on these pages. We have started this journey together with me being transparent in my feelings and experiences and I want you to do the same. When you put your thoughts and notes right on the pages, you are able to reference them later and know exactly what it was that brought you to that thought.

We will have some journaling, a few assessments, some affirmations and then we will create your new Self Standard together. While you are writing, I want you to use "I statements," so you take ownership and FEEL your words. You are not allowed to use the words "can't" or "try," I mean, it's not like I will be able to actually see it, so we are just going to go with the honor system, okay? If you got it, say, "I got it!" Okay, okay try that again because I know you read it but you didn't SAY IT and I need you to SAY IT! So if you got it say, "I got it!" Much better! Thank you! Now let's do this!

Introduction

A few years ago, I turned 30. In my mind, I was living my life at its *peak*. I was driving my dream car, Delta Airlines had become my Uber and remembering payday was a thing of the past. If you asked me then how things were, my answer would have been a resounding, *"I'm living the dream."* Two years into that dreamlife, it all came to a screeching halt. I lost my job, my six-year relationship, my car, my home and worst of all, my will to keep going. I fell out of love with the person I've known since birth; me. There were a few friends who stuck around and tried to keep me encouraged, but it still wasn't enough. I woke up one day and realized that losing so much hurt so bad because in those moments they were the things that kept me motivated.

It took quite some time to find a job, I had to move back in with my parents after a full adulthood of freedom. I was back living in the room I grew up in, but in a completely different phase in life. I felt like a failure, undesirable and worthless. I was masking my daily routine with smiles and colorful commentary. Inside I was crumbling and hoping no one would realize just how awful I felt.

I was hopping from job to job, taking on new endeavors and industries hoping to fill the void and ache in my heart when I looked at myself daily. I'd moved from sales, to long- term unemployment, to retail, on to collections, then customer service, back to sales, finally landing in shipping and logistics. Constantly chasing a feeling, I didn't know if I'd ever find again, the feeling of relevancy and status.

I felt awkward in seemingly normal situations. Thoughts ran through my head constantly of what people thought of me, now that I had been stripped of everything that I thought made someone, "successful." I tried keeping a smile on my face and determination as my springboard. I looked for things I could do or start to regain financial footing and kept coming up short.

I spent years and thousands of dollars investing in personal and professional development only for each of those principles to be forgotten in an instant. Vanished like smoke in the wind when I needed those teachings the most. While I had repeated fleeting thoughts of terminating my existence, I never could bring myself to discuss with others, or seek help, for fear of appearing "weak," or "dramatic."

In February of 2017, I became extremely ill. My body was shutting down, probably because I stopped caring for it. Less than 30 days later, I was diagnosed with jaundice. After MONTHS of testing; blood work, MRIs, ultrasounds and appointments, my doctors didn't know what was causing it. My skin turned leathery, much like beef jerky and dry. I had these tiny pimples everywhere. My eyes were the color of brand-new highlighters. My self-esteem hit a low I've never experienced before. I felt ugly and worthless. I avoided cameras and mirrors like a vampire. If I was captured on film, I begged to be filtered only in black and white. I realized then, even though my life didn't feel like it was worth living, I wasn't ready to die.

With reservations and yet a sliver of hope, I decided to keep pressing on.

Acting "the part" had never been a difficult thing for me, but then one night after coming home from my new job as an overnight supervisor for a large shipping and logistics company, I realized I needed more. I couldn't keep living day in and day out worried what someone else thought of me, my situation or my life. I had to take the reins and start loving to look at the reflection and feel a sense of pride. From these dark times, this book was born.

I chose the title *#ImpressYourself* because it only took me a split moment to realize I had been so unhappy for so long because I wasn't living for ME. I was trying to fill the shoes of who other people saw or knew me to be, but I wasn't living my authentic self.

Writing this book has been a therapeutic journey. Being able to share details that I wouldn't dare admit out loud before, and now presenting them to you has shown me that I am finally doing things I want to do for *me*, unapologetically.

As you pass through these pages, your circumstances may not be as vivid as mine, they may be more extreme or less; but the fact that you're here says you're ready to take some steps to create a person YOU can fall, or stay in love, with. I want us to have a conversation. Some of the conversations and prompts may be triggering, but they are to help you break through to your *best* self! Let's get started! I'm Candace, and it's nice to meet you.

#GetToKnowYou

"If we're really honest with ourselves, most of us will admit that we want to impress people, and this is what is causing us to do what we do."

-*Joyce Meyer*

Who are you? Not what you look like, not what other people call you. Who are you to your core? Before we get into the heavy stuff, let's take a little assessment and see which category of YOU, you identify with the most.

1. This book was purchased by:

    a. Me

    b. Someone gave it to me as a gift

2. I feel most comfortable and confident:

    a. In a group

    b. Being alone

3. I am most excited when:

    a. I am finishing something

    b. I am starting something

4. I feel most accomplished when:

    a. I feel good about what I have done

    b. Someone tells me they feel good about what I have done

5. I feel the need to be recognized for:

    a. How I make people feel

    b. Things I do for people

6. I find myself thinking about:

    a. What impact I have made during a situation

    b. What people think about me after a situation

7. I tend to compare myself to:

    a. Former versions of myself

    b. Other people

8. I consider myself:

    a. Encouraged to finish my goals in spite of what people think of them

    b. Easily distracted from my goals based on what people think of them

9. I share my goals with:

    a. People who help me stay accountable to my goals

    b. No one, because not everyone wishes the best for you

10. I exercise self-care when I need it:

    a. Frequently

    b. Not usually, but I think about it

Do you identify more with A or B answers? If you identified more with A, you are already well on your way to impressing yourself. If you identified more with B, this book is perfect for you to start that journey to impressing YOU. First let me congratulate you for taking a step towards giving yourself permission to be unapologetically and authentically YOU. Aooow!

Let's break down the questions from our assessment. If you bought this book for yourself, what was it about *this* book that made you want to pick it up? If it was a gift, why do you think it was purchased for you? Jot down a few things you hope to enhance by reading this book, (we'll be using these later so get to writing).

____

____

____

____

Now that was easier than you thought right? Good, let's keep going. So, talk to me about being comfortable and confident. Which one did you choose, in a group or being alone? What is it about the opposite of what you chose that you don't like? Write down what you like about your choice and write a few things you don't like about the opposite choice.

____

____

____

____

Terms we hear with these two instances are usually extroverted and introverted, or you could very well be an ambivert, (which means both). You are allowed to have mixed feelings and it could easily be based on situations and circumstances. Before I started taking steps in my journey, I didn't find myself comfortable or confident being alone. Mostly because I felt that I was so hard on myself and my thoughts would consume me. It was much easier to be "on" in a group; where I could use charm and wit to distract from how I was really feeling day in and day out.

The hardest part about being by yourself, in my experience, was everywhere I went, I was there too. I couldn't escape me. I have learned how to find a balance, but not until there came a time in my life where I realized I never even lived alone. From birth, I have always cohabited with someone. From my parents and sister, to roommates in college, to partners; someone was always around, giving me their opinion of what I could be, or should be doing.

Okay, so you remember the breakup I told you about? Yeah that. I was in that relationship for six years and then it crumbled. I was left to figure things out on my own. I had to move back in with my parents, (mostly for financial reasons) and I was right back to living with someone again. Over some time, I was able to get back on my feet and move out on my own. This time it *was* by myself. At 33 years old, I was living on my own for the first time in my life.

I remember watching my best friend purchase her house a few years before that, she was living alone and just so free. I, on the other hand, felt caged and afraid. When I moved into my house, I couldn't sleep through the night for like the first two weeks. No I wasn't scared of the dark or anything. I was afraid of me. I was scared the silence would engulf me and I didn't know what to do with that. I wasn't comfortable or confident in my ability to sustain myself; emotionally or financially. After those two weeks, I couldn't take it anymore and I started looking at the perks of being alone.

I could decorate without anyone's input. I would only buy the foods I like to eat. I can leave my shoes by the door for days and no one is going to complain, except me when I trip over them. Being alone and really getting to spend time with myself has taught me how to be in groups and *not* feel the need to be "on" or almost mask myself. I'll tell you more later about some of the things I've done while being alone to get to know myself and find that confidence.

Alright, back to this assessment. Wait, how about this? Whenever I'm going to give you an instance of a personal experience, I'll say, "**Story Time**" first. That way you can just sit back and enjoy. How does that sound? Well I'm doing it anyway :)

Ok the assessment. What kinds of things excite you? Is it starting something? Are you the type who jumps feet first into a project and figure it out along the way, (sometimes never finishing it), or are you more of the person who plans things out, gets started and sees it all the way through to completion? In my opinion, it's really easy to birth an idea or project and it all makes perfect sense when you first brainstorm. The implementation can seem like the difficult part. Things come up, obstacles get in the way, or you run out of time. I mean seriously, have you been on Pinterest lately?

Think about five things you've started, *for you* that you haven't finished yet: why did you start the project and why haven't you finished? Was it a home decor project? Was it planning a trip? How about a new hobby? You tell me, and really think about what it was that stopped you from finishing it? Was it not coming out the way you thought it would? Did it get too hard? Too time consuming? Did you get distracted and start something else? Of those five things tell me about two.

____

____

____

____

____

____

____

____

____

Now that you got that out, I bet you want to go back to it and start on it again, don't you? I know you do. That's natural. Ok, so on the flipside, think about five things you finished. Tell me about three of them. What was it? How did you finish them? I'll even allow something you haven't finished but are still actively working on. Now, this is where it gets hard because usually, we magnify the things we don't do and minimize the things we accomplish. So, I don't care how small you think it is, if you finished it, tell me about it. While you write, I want you to think about how you felt when you got to the end of the task/project. Now also tell me how you felt when you finished it. I'm going to give you more space for this one, because around here we CELEBRATE the wins! Annnd Go!

Now that we have some accomplishments written down, let's talk about how it felt. Did you feel more accomplished because of *what* you did or because someone positively commented on it? We all need positive reinforcement. Living in the age of social media we can get that pretty instantly, right? Make a post, get likes, comments and shares. Doesn't it feel really good to get those likes? It can, but didn't it feel better to *do* what you posted about?

To me, social media is a gift and a curse. It's a very useful tool to stay connected in a world of technology, but it also gives us a "highlight reel," into the lives of others. You have some people who post some of their struggles, but typically you see the good, not the bad or the ugly. It can be really easy to start to size yourself up against those posts. We live in a society of reality tv, and instant access into the, "behind the scenes," of people's lives, but it's still all only what they want you to know.

A friend recently asked me, why do I post so much on social media? When I thought about it, my first mind took me to the "memories" that sites give you. I like to see the steps I've taken and what's gotten me here. Most often I post because something resonated with me in the moment and because it was relevant. Other times I post what I think "future me" needs to see from where we are today. Facebook has this feature called "*Memories on This Day.*"

I like being able to look back on where I was one year, three years, even 10 years ago and see what's changed for me or what's stayed the same. Oddly, I remember seeing a post I wrote nearly 10 years prior to writing this book, saying, "I want to write a book." It was a reminder of ideas and aspirations I had inside of me that sometimes gets lost in the hustle of daily life, like we spoke about in our question about starting things, but not finishing them. Sometimes, ideas are seeds and don't have to be completed at the moment, and other times you have to take advantage of bringing them to life in the season they are available.

What have you most recently accomplished? And what have you most recently been recognized for accomplishing?

____

____

____

____

____

____

____

____

____

Speaking of recognition, I once was told that recognition is the gratification babies cry for and grown men die for. From as far back as we can remember, we have craved recognition in some form. Whether that was gold stars for doing chores, paychecks and promotions, or even down to a shout out on social media, we as a culture, crave recognition. There is nothing wrong with being recognized or wanting recognition for things you have done, but my question is; what are you still willing to do even if you never get the recognition you desire or deserve from others?

Feeling the recognition from within first, allows you to have a sense of pride regardless of if anyone notices or not. Imagine you have built a table; you sit back and stare at it proudly. I come to your home and say, "Wow this is a really nice table where did you get it from?" You start to feel warm inside as the comparison of the table you were nervous about building, is noticed, and compared to a table that would have been purchased. You get the warm feeling because you are not a carpenter by trade, so it is not normal for you to build tables especially a good one. You would have built the table anyway because you needed it, however the recognition from someone else gives you just a little bit more pleasure and pride.

When I finally was able to answer that question, my life transformed exponentially. Our assessment asked if you like to be recognized for how you make people feel or the things you can do for them. These may seem similar, but they are very different. When you make someone *feel* something, they may not always recognize you publicly. You may never be told you made them feel something. From childhood we were taught, no ingrained, to say thank you when someone does something for us. Can you hear your mom's voice now saying, "Now what do you say?" and you follow with your sheepish response of, "Thank you."

It's been drilled into us since we could speak, to say thank you. I'm not speaking down on acknowledging things, or being grateful for something, I'm simply saying we have been saying thank you, without even really knowing why for about 90% of our lives. Now we want some sense of recognition or validation when we do something. It's a level of reinforcement; and moreover, it FEELS good.

Have you ever heard about Pavlov's dogs? Here is the gist of it; he would ring the bell during meal times and it caused the dogs to salivate, and because he coupled them together for a specified amount of time, he was able to condition the dogs to salivate at the sound of the bell even if there was no food. Over time, we have conditioned ourselves with recognition and sometimes start to seek it even with minimal effort. What is it about recognition that you feel you need? What does it feel like to you?

Hey, guess what time it is? Yup, Story Time!

Most of my life I have been considered (by other people), as an overachiever. Now did I get perfect grades in school? Uh nah, not me. Was I the best on my teams when I played sports? Nope, try again. Was I the smartest? Wrong again. I think most of my life I have been pretty average as far as those types of metrics go, however, I was always the kid who did things without complaint and with ease. I grew up a military brat. We moved state to state every two-three years, and each time we moved, I had a chance to reinvent myself.

In those reinventions, I realized I was taking pieces of what worked one place and remodeling it to fit my new location and surroundings. I wasn't being myself per se because I didn't really know what that was. I was being the best version of what I was recognized for. I was recognized for being a hard worker, someone who had good ideas, and being a team player.

I was a team player because it was easier to fall in line when you were always the new girl. So, was I really a team player, or was I just agreeable? My mom, who was a stay at home mom, spent a lot of time investing into me and my sister. She put me specifically in a lot of artsy related activities like acting, speaking and dance. Those activities taught me to pick up on things quickly and adapt almost immediately to new situations and scenarios. It taught me how to think on my feet as an adult. I took a strong liking to these things. But as I got older, it started making me more recognizable by people, I didn't (then) see the value in being recognized by. I had a natural talent, so I didn't see it as work and the people I wanted to be friends with, didn't see it as cool.

Now, name one pre-teen or teenage girl who *wants* to be not only the new girl, but the new weird girl? I'll wait. Yeah, I couldn't think of anyone either. I started seeking recognition from my peers who had no real substance when it came to what was worth being recognized for. Eventually, I stopped seeking the recognition from my peers and started wanting to wake up saying I was proud of me for what I have been able to do. We are going to talk more about it later, so keep this in mind. Some would call itself serving, however, we live in a polar universe, so if we aren't serving self, the opposite would be serving, (and I don't mean in a Biblical, Samaritan kind of way), others. I noticed when I started doing things that made *me* feel proud, recognition started coming more frequently and from places and people I least expected it from. I started walking in my own truth and patting myself on the back.

When is the last time you felt recognized? Who recognized you? How did you respond to the recognition emotionally? Are there any other things that give you that same emotional feeling?

____

____

____

____

____

Oh you need more space? Here you go.

____

____

____

____

____

____

____

____

____

Since we are already on the subject of feelings and emotions, let's go to our next question which was what you think about. In most of your interactions with people, do you find yourself thinking about the impact you left or more about what they think about you? We all have that voice in our head. It's your thinking voice. It's that voice that pops in every now and again during situations. Okay, so scenario: you're out to lunch with an associate; not a close friend, but someone you're friendly with. Conversation is flowing, vibes are good and you're both enjoying the meal. Are you more worried about what you look like at the table versus what you bring to the table? Our insecurities can sometimes take over and be overwhelming, especially when around a new person. Are you in the moment with them, or is your mind wandering, thinking about your outfit, and hair?

Now that may seem like a silly example, but it happens; daily for some, multiple times for others. Oh, not you? Ok cool. Yeah, I didn't believe you either. Because we all have had moments, maybe not *exactly* like this one, but something similar. It's my belief that it's natural to have fleeting thoughts, but when they become overbearing or debilitating, that's when it can become dangerous.

Are you spending more time worried about what other people are thinking about you rather than engaging with them and letting them have their feelings about you no matter what they may be? Have you ever heard someone make a comment about someone else saying, "I just don't like them," and the reason being, "I don't know, I just don't." Yeah, I've heard it before too, and someone has probably said it about you, and you don't know it.

The amazing thing about that is it doesn't really matter when you are secure in *you* and know that each day you step foot into this world you are bringing your best self. It's not your job to make people like you. It's your job to *be* you. But how can you bring your best self if you are still questioning who that best self is? That's step one, and by the end of our journey together, I want you to have a better sense of who that is.

Impact is all you can control. You can control what you bring as a value to a situation and/or conversation. I have adopted the mentality that I want people to have positive feelings after an encounter with me. I do this by actively listening to people, remembering details they have shared with me and asking them questions. In turn, it allows me to learn more about them, but it also gives me a chance to quiet that little voice, that may want to make an appearance every now and again with insecurities and doubts about myself. We are all a work in progress and should always be evolving and growing, so these feelings again are natural. However, you can control them and choose what you listen to or not.

In this same vein, question seven asked about making comparisons between our "old self" and other people. There is a meme floating around social media that says, "One of the greatest tragedies in life is to lose your own sense of self and accept the version of you that *is* expected by everyone else." I believe the only comparison you have a right to make is with yourself. I say that because no one's situation is exactly like yours. No one's experience is exactly like yours. There are things that have happened to you and for you in a very intricate design that is specific to only you.

There is no way to truly make a comparison of yourself to others. DNA alone tells us we are all very unique and our experiences can only be attributed to our behavior and surroundings. Think about how you approach situations. If you just have an inherent need to examine your life against someone else's, you have to ask yourself some very real questions. Are you doing what's necessary to attain those things this person has, (if they are "better than" your situation)? Conversely, what have you done to maintain and sustain what you have and who you are compared to someone who is "worse off" than you?

I want you to brag on yourself right now. I want to know a few things about you now versus the old you. I'm going to let you pick the time frame, because I can testify even a year can make a huge difference in growth, or demise, for that matter. In this exercise, we want to focus on the growth. Pick two moments in time, one being the present day and the other being some time before. And I want you to write a letter to *that* you. I want you to write it telling that older version of yourself what you are doing in life now that you didn't think you could by this point.

What was the old you afraid of, that you have overcome? What adventures have you had as the new you that seemed impossible as the old you? Remember those accomplishments we talked about earlier? You can use some of those as examples in your letter to the old you. Write this letter explaining to the old you how excited you are that they are where they are now, to get you to where you are now, even if that transition doesn't feel like leaps and bounds. Did the old you not know how to cook, and the new you learned a new recipe? Did the old you have a habit that the new you doesn't have anymore? Did the old you have a hard time with something that now is easier to do for the new you? You see where I'm going with this, okay I'll be quiet, shhh, you write. I'll be right over here.

Dear ____

It's me, the NEW you, I just wanted to write you and let you know.

____

____

____

____

____

____

____

____

____

____

____

____

____

Love Always, _______________________________________

Date ______________________

How did that feel? See you can't compare that to anyone else because that is *you*. You did that. You made that happen. You learned that thing. Oooh later we'll actually write a letter to your FUTURE self, that could be fun!

When you write that letter to your future self, I want you to keep in mind your answer for number eight and number nine, (it's a two-for-one special)! Goal setting can be difficult for some, and that's usually if you don't have an idea of why you have a goal or what you are aiming for, and you have no way to measure the goal. I'll give you some tools to help with that a little later. I want to talk now about the feeling you have towards the goals you have set now. When you set a goal, is it something you truly want to accomplish or something you *think* you are supposed to want.

Society has done a fantastic job of pretty much telling us what we are supposed to want or have in life. How we should feel about those goals and if you aren't at a certain place by a certain age, then you have basically failed. But your timeline is YOUR timeline. So when you set goals do you usually tell people who are close to you? People who know your habits, (or at least your old habits, because together we are going to be creating some new ones). Do they encourage you and check in on you during your progress? Do they support you? Are they invested in seeing you reach those goals? (Support is a verb, so you have to know what kind of support you need as well - it's ok if you don't know at this second, I'll help you with that too).

What does support look like to you? Are you honest with what you need or how you need to feel supported? If you find you are easily, or often, distracted from your goals, I want us to talk about that too. Not distracted in the sense of it's taking you longer than expected, but you are still actively working on it. I'm more so talking about the kind of distracted where you forget about the goal altogether and jump onto something else. If you find that happens to you often, it could very well be that the goal didn't have a significant enough reason for you to stick with it. What motivates you to get it done? Please above all don't say money. I say that because if it were really about money, well we'd all be rich I'm sure. What significance does the goal have for you? What will be the result once you have obtained or reached the goal?

Tell me about 5-7 goals you have. You don't need to go into too much detail in this moment, but we will use these later and break down HOW to get those things done, by finding the internal source that will help you get there.

1. ____

2. ____

3. ____

4. ____

5. ____

6. ____

7. ____

Doesn't it feel good to see them written out? I really like number 4 on your list. Nice!

Hey, you're doing awesome, I know it's been a good bit of writing so far. I hope you didn't use a gel pen, that may bleed through the pages. I should have said something earlier. Well, if you are using a gel pen and it's not bothering you, it's not bothering me. If you were using a gel pen, I bet you changed it after the first line of writing, I know I would have.

We only have one more thing to talk about from our assessment, self-care. One of the most widely talked about subjects, but also so very much ignored. Because we may talk about things that could be triggering, I want to be clear that you have at least the foundation of a self-care plan. What types of things do you currently do for self-care? It should be any activity that you deliberately do to take care of your emotional, mental and physical health.

It is also a catalyst to a good relationship with yourself and others. It should be something that refuels you, not something you are reluctant or hesitant to do. It should be actively planned not just circumstantial and keep your commitment to yourself to do it. Self-care can often be seen as and feel like a reward, and in turn feel like something that is optional, or replaceable. It is an active choice and should be treated as such. It will mean different things to different people.

Personally, I lead a very busy life between a career, running a small business and having an active social life, as well as being an author. Something that I do each and every week for myself without fail is keep Sunday to myself. I don't book anything outside of family related events for Sunday. My favorite part about my Self Care Sunday, is Second Sleep.

Second Sleep is when you wake up earlier than you planned, go have breakfast and then take that extra nap. That extra nap is the best thing to ever happen to me. It allows me to reset and feel refreshed to start my week all over again. Here is an example of my full Self Care plan:

Emotional/Mental Self Care: When I find myself in need of an emotional break, I sit quietly for 10-15 minutes and listen to music. Usually a few songs from one of my preloaded Pandora stations. If in a very tight moment I find myself feeling anxious or unfocused, I pull out my phone and play two to three turns of a game. This usually helps me refocus my energy and whatever was weighing heavily on my mind or emotions starts to evaporate and I can think more levelheaded. Creating work that is just free flowing is helpful when I feel either stuck or just intense emotions, so painting is an outlet for me. Journaling is also something I rely heavily on as a way to express myself and mental energy.

Social Self Care: I live alone, so I exercise myself care socially by calling a friend and talking for a few. I usually do this while doing another mindless task such as folding clothes or cleaning the house. Talking on the phone allows me to connect to people as this is something I know I require, while still being able to take care of other personal needs as well. I maintain a standing appointment with a few friends at least on a monthly basis, to get out and meet in person and not focus on work or my business.

Physical Self Care: As I described earlier Sunday Second Sleep is my absolute favorite self-care activity. I reserve that time just for me. As a person who is activity heavy, I like to take some full days of downtime at least twice a month, where I will rest, and just relax my mind and body by catching up on my favorite shows or taking in a new movie.

Emergency Self Care: There can come a time where I have become emotionally charged past my breaking point. My notification that I have reached that place is usually when my ears get really hot and throat feels tight. At this point my emergency plan is to take a few deep breaths and pace. I find a single point to focus my eyes on and breathe until I can feel my mood change.

Spiritual Self Care: Along with my emotional/mental self-care, I also practice Spiritual self-care by reading my Bible app, when I feel in a fog. I pray nightly, typically for clarity and guidance. I also start most days with meditation and thankful thoughts. When I feel spiritually heavy, I will engage in fasting usually from alcohol for a few days at a time. This typically makes my head and my heart clearer and lighter.

If you have an active Self Care plan, list one or two activities you consciously do for self-care?

____

____

____

____

____

____

____

____

____

If you don't currently have a self-care plan, what is one activity you can start with this week for self-care? What is something you can do today?

____

____

____

____

____

____

____

____

I have given you some examples of my self-care plan. Here you will find a template for you to start your own if you don't already have one, or you'd like to update what you currently do. The plan is broken into categories to help you guide your activities through different stages.

Sample Self Care Plan

1. Physical- (e.g. eating habits, exercise, sleep patterns)
2. Emotional- (e.g. self-expression, positive activities)
3. Spiritual- (e.g. inspirational readings, meditation)
4. Social- (e.g. relationships, schedules)
5. Mental- (e.g. journaling, reading)
6. Emergency- (e.g. music, focus points)

Use these prompts as ways to start creating your plan and begin to implement it in your daily routine.

Wow, that didn't take that long at all. How do you feel?! That assessment isn't any peer reviewed, clinical, or psychological assessment of personality. It was designed as a gauge for us and a way to get your brain flowing and working with YOU as the subject. While you go through the rest of this book, it's my suggestion to take it chapter by chapter and put a few days to a week in between reading each chapter. This isn't designed as a "quick read," or "fast fix."

I want you to really take the time to dig into these entries with your thoughts and emotions. Dig deep because we'll have to get to the root to be able to help you manifest into the you, you are destined to be. I would say I'm impressed with you right now, but you should already have a least a hint of feeling impressed with yourself.

#NoPondLife

"We judge ourselves by our intentions, and others by their actions."
-Stephen R. Covey

Let's start off with an exercise. I want you to stand up. Go ahead, physically stand up. Ok, now sit down. Now try to stand up. Did you hesitate a little? You probably did hesitate because you can't *try* to stand up, you either stand or your sit/fall. When speaking of actions there is no way to "try" you either do it or you don't.

"There is no try, only do." -Yoda

Let's discuss intentions and actions. By definition, intention, a noun, means "an act or instance of determining mentally upon some action or result." So often we intend to do something. We think about it for days, weeks, months or years before we take action. I like to consider this paralysis of analysis. Other words related to intention are aim, hope, motive, objective, plan and design. All of these words are useful and even necessary, however not one of these words gets anything done.

Think about the last time you had a lazy day. A day where you *intended* to get the laundry done, clean the house and run some much needed, but not emergent errands. While these were your *plans, objectives,* and *hopes;* your decision ultimately dictated your actions which did not yield the desired results. Even though these weren't life or death situations you decided not do, how did you feel at the end of the day? You find that the sun has gone down, and you are on your 10th episode of your current Netflix binge?

What was your self-talk? Did you beat yourself up? It may sound a little like this, "Is it really 8 o'clock? The whole day is gone. I was supposed to get so much done today. This is going to make my week so much harder." I get it, we are busy people and our intentions don't always lead us to the actions we anticipated. If you have gone down that path and gave yourself the negative talk, what does the opposite look like? "It's really 8 o'clock, I had a really refreshing day and that was a good show. I'm glad I was able to take today to watch it and get some rest."

In the chapter quote, Stephen Covey says we judge others by their actions and ourselves by our intentions. It's much easier to give yourself a pass. Here is an example: you are hosting a free event. You are providing all supplies, snacks and entertainment. You have excellent marketing and have asked people to preregister for your event, so you know how much to have on hand. The day of the event arrives and of the 50 people who pre-registered, only three have shown up.

Of course, you are upset at first, because they said they were coming. They even filled out the form to make sure they had a spot at the event. You have purchased all these items to make sure the event was a success and the feeling of disappointment starts to form. You question why didn't they come? You begin to blame other events that may be going on, or the weather. But do you ever stop in that moment to think of all the events you may have signed up for and *intended* to go to, but didn't show up? You gave yourself a pass for your own actions, but in turn are holding your non attendees to the fire. Why do we find excuses for ourselves and not hold ourselves to the same level of accountability?

We tend to make concessions for ourselves because it is easier to know our intentions without the need to explain. We know we mean well, we know the details of our thought patterns, but we must find a way to convey that to others. What makes sense to us without explanation or reason doesn't always make sense to others. Taking an internal evaluation becomes important. We must take a look at our reflection and see what our actions portray not to others, but to ourselves. We don't take into account that we are letting ourselves down each time we neglect to keep a commitment. We hold others accountable to us because we see ourselves as important enough that *they* should keep their commitment to us. The accountability becomes lost because we aren't seeing ourselves as important enough to keep a commitment to.

When I started acting on my intentions, I noticed a shift in my overall happiness. I no longer had to look for excuses as to why I couldn't attend an event I said I would go to, but I also stopped agreeing to do things I didn't really want to do. We all have done it. I am guilty myself. When I started saying no to more things I didn't want to do, I found myself able to start saying yes to things I did like, and my intentions stopped being plans. Once I learned more about myself, what my true likes and dislikes were, and I stopped doing things to get a return from someone, I became happier.

Here is an exercise. Look at your calendar of events for the next 90 days between work/business, social and home life. Categorize the activities into two columns, Interests and Commitments. In the interest column, I want you to add the items you have there that you said you would do that you are not fully vested in. For the commitment's column, add the items you must do, or you are very excited about doing.

<u>Interests</u>   <u>Commitments</u>

_______________   _______________

_______________   _______________

_______________   _______________

_______________   _______________

_______________   _______________

_______________   _______________

_______________   _______________

What do you notice about this list? Is your Interests column larger than your Commitments column? Are there any interests that can become commitments? Are there commitments you could convert to interests? When I took a broader look at what I was committing myself to and made a shift, I felt less stressed. I felt less anxious, and less like I would let someone down. I used to struggle with how I was perceived by people and because I wanted to be liked and accepted, I would commit to things that were oftentimes not even interests. While involved in the event I would be unhappy, disengaged and almost annoyed. I was still always pleasant of course, but I would go home feeling drained because I had to work harder to enjoy myself. There are some activities you cannot get away from, usually with work or home/family events, so for those I suggest finding a way to turn them from interests into commitments.

Intentions are not bad, they set the framework for our actions, but let's talk about how we make that transition. Action is a verb and by definition means, "something done or performed." If intention is the cause, action is the effect. Actions are fed by the results we get. I like to think of it like this:

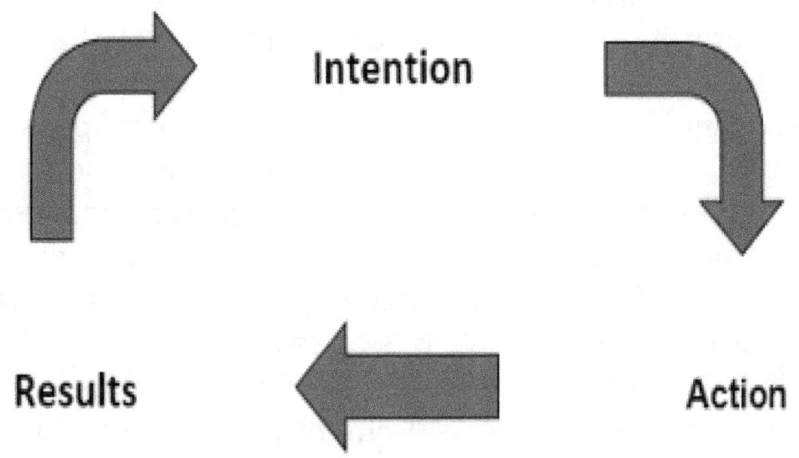

Everything starts with the intention, or the desire to do it. From there, you must perform the action to start getting results. The more you see results, the more your desire and intention grows. This is how you can transform items and events from interests to commitments. The first example that comes to mind is weight loss. We have all seen how this works, and if the intention was enough, we'd all have "perfect" bodies.

There are so many tools out there to get the results we want, but where the chain is broken is the action. There are pills, potions, wraps, trainers, gyms and programs. Some people use these tactics effectively and the results are there. Other times, you can use these tools and the results are not there. Now the action starts to dwindle. Can someone say January through March at your local Planet Fitness? **Guess what time it is?! Story Time!**

A few years back, I was at the heaviest weight I had ever been. My lifestyle, while fabulous, was pretty sedentary for most of the day. I had a sales job and spent the better part of eight hours tethered to a computer and affixed on a computer screen. When I lost my job that January, that sedentary lifestyle increased as getting out of the bed didn't seem like an option most days. The easiest things to eat came out of a box or a can, I was so unhappy, and it was starting to show in my body not just my emotions. My partner at the time would call me a picture frame, as I was usually in the exact same place and space from the time she left for work and when she came home. I knew I needed to do something, but I used the excuse of not working as a way to justify not spending the money for a membership somewhere. My intention was there, and I would lay around daily loathing how I looked and trying to will myself to get up and get moving.

One afternoon, I was getting dressed to go look for a job and my pants did not button with as much ease as they did six months ago. At that moment I knew, it was either buy a whole new wardrobe or start to drop some weight.

My *reason* for losing weight changed, so my intention became stronger. I researched a few gyms, and finally settled on one that had a free trial and an option for a session with a personal trainer and a nutritionist. I got up to the gym for the first time and met the trainer. He was encouraging and asked me more questions about me than my weight, this made me feel like he really wanted to help me and not just add me to his roster.

I made a commitment to attend sessions with him once a week for 30 minutes. He gave me a meal plan, I followed it concisely and with excitement because I wanted to see the change. I wasn't skeptical once I started. I truly believed that my actions would yield the results as long as I kept doing them. At first, it was small changes I noticed. I wasn't as winded going up the stairs. I could see my face slimming down in the mirror. I kept working at it. I was excited and energized by the results I was getting. Over time as my form was getting better, we had to add more weight to my regimen, and I was getting faster with my cardio.

Within 90 days, I was down over 30 pounds and felt better than I had in years. My clothes fit better, I had more energy, I could look in the mirror and be proud of what my body was transforming to. I kept working out because I got the results I wanted and in what I considered a reasonable time. I eventually stopped going to the trainer, I learned what I needed to be able to do to maintain the results where I wanted them. I was impressed with how far I had come.

The key here is to not just have intentions, but to *move* with intention as well. Have a purpose when you do things. When your purpose is strong enough, the desired action and results begin to come. Have you ever noticed when you stop just thinking about an idea and actually start moving into action on that idea, it breeds more action and results? A few friends and I affectionately call this the, *"No Pond Life."*

Pond water is stagnant and stale. It is sitting water that breeds bacteria and not much grows from it. But moving water; rivers, creeks, brooks even, you see lots of action around them. Plants growing, wildlife flourishing, and earth literally being moved due to the constant movement of the water. So, make a promise to yourself to live a, *"No Pond Life."*

I want you to think of your own example. What is something you have been struggling with either in the intention, action, or result? Write them here in the spaces below:

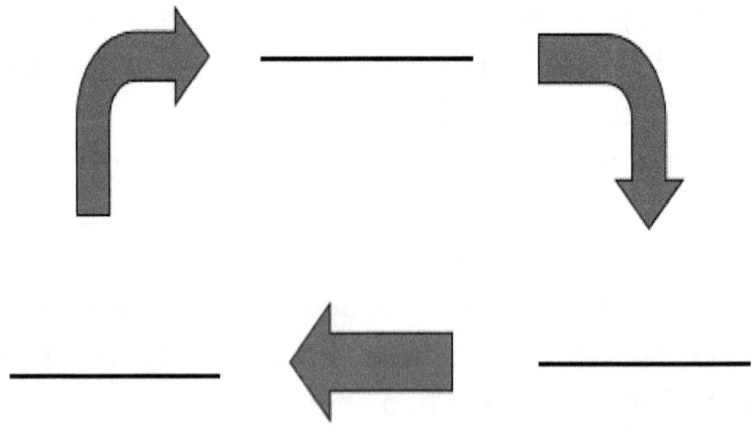

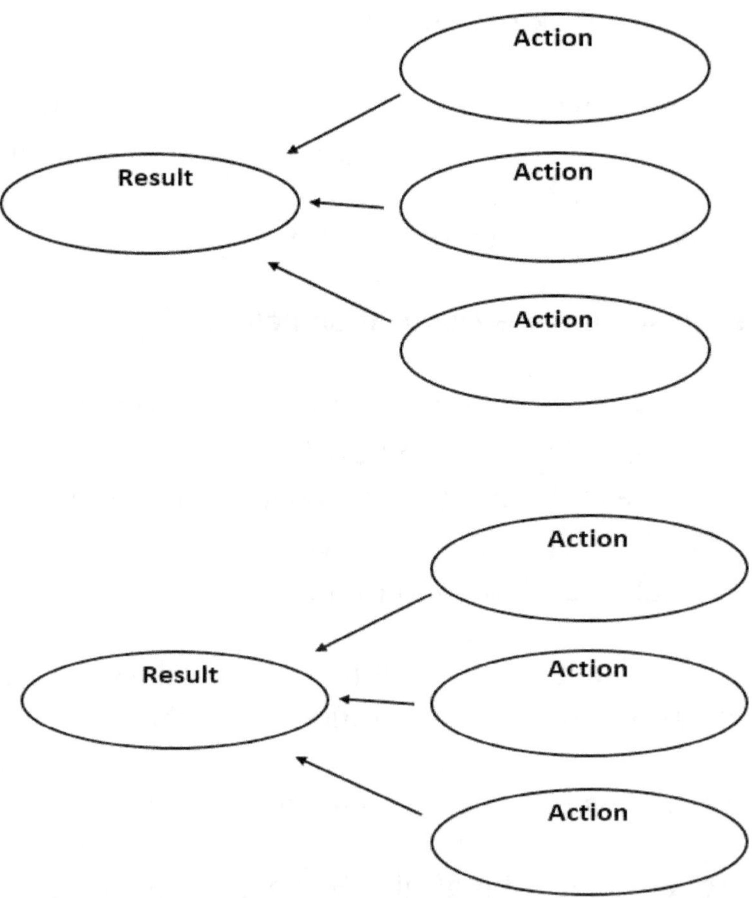

From what you have created here, let's list some action steps you have already taken, and brainstorm some new ones, to get you to the results you want. We will work this step backwards. I find it easier at times to know the end result and then figure out how to get there. For example, if you are talking about weight loss, the result would be, lose 10 pounds. The action to accompany that can be meal prepping, join a gym, find an accountability partner and decide the number of times you will work out per week.

When you speak, does it feel like people don't believe you? If you make a declaration of sorts, is it often questioned or given the eye roll? Some of that could come from previous behavior of lots of intention, but very little action. If you are the person who is known for, "talking a good game," but not following through, today is the day you can begin to change that.

Here are some steps that can be helpful:

1. Speak with conviction each and every time.
2. When you say you are going to do something, mean it and do it. Be a person of your word.
3. Only commit to activities and ideas you are absolutely willing to do.

Speak it, mean it and commit to it. If you take your actions and ideas and pass them through these three filters, you can start building other's belief in you and more importantly, your belief in yourself.

We are allowed to be afraid. However, just because you are afraid doesn't mean you have to show it or let it stop you. When you speak, especially about something for yourself, speak with a belief so strong that others have no choice, but to believe in you as well, (this is reinforced when you are consistent with number two). It can be hard to say no to friends and family when they want us to be a part of something but saying no when you aren't fully vested or interested, can save a lot of hurt feelings for yourself and them later on. It's better to step up now and say no so that you can maintain numbers one and two on your journey.

Most importantly, today stops the language of, "I had every intention to..." From today forward, you either do something or you don't. Own up to your actions and you will see the behavior change. If you decide *not* to do something, that is okay too. Speak it, mean it and commit to it. Think about this, what are some motivators to keep you going in your commitments?

52

#ImpressYourself

#NoMoreSnoozeButton

"People often say that motivation doesn't last. Well, neither does bathing - that's why we recommend it daily."

-Zig Ziglar

You may have heard the question, "What's your W.H.Y.?" Instances of this phrase being used are typically to discover what motivates you. What gets you up in the morning? I'm not talking about your alarm clock, or am I? Motivation can be compared to an alarm clock. When it sounds off, it prompts you to spring into action. Today, we stop pressing snooze! Let's go back to the question of, "What's your W.H.Y.?" W.H.Y. is an acronym that can be used in two ways, **W**hat **H**urts **Y**ou or **W**hat **H**elps/**H**eals **Y**ou.

Motivation by definition is a verb and means a cause or reason to act. Again, your alarm clock. You can have one of two types of alarm clocks: an internal and an external. I'm here to tell you, everything you need to be, you already are, you just need to stop hitting the snooze button on your alarm.

Let me give you two scenarios. Visualize this with me, close your eyes. Imagine you have been saving most of your life for your dream vacation. Wait, open your eyes, you can't keep reading with your eyes closed. Ok let's try again. You have saved up for your dream vacation, you are all packed and have a 6:00am flight and an alarm set for 3:00am. BZZZ the alarm goes off at 3:00am and you pop up without hitting snooze and no hesitation, get yourself dressed and off to the airport. Separate scenario. You have had a job you're good at, but don't really like for years now. You make a pretty good salary, but lack fulfillment at work.

It's Monday morning after a holiday weekend and you have your alarm set for 6:00am to be to work by 8:30am. BZZZ the alarm goes off, you hit the snooze button until 6:15am. BZZZ the alarm goes off again, you hit the snooze button again until 6:30am. BZZZ once again the alarm goes off and you snooze it until 7:00am. You finally turn off the alarm and just lay there. You think about your bills, and how many sick days you have left and decide to get up and get dressed and just barely make it in the office before 8:30am.

Do you see the difference between the two scenarios? In our first scenario, there is excitement, dedication and internal motivation. Nothing was going to get in the way of waking up on time and getting on that plane. In the reverse, the second scenario. Well there was an allowance for anything to come in the way, but ultimately you made it to work, likely due to external motivation. In most instances, a paycheck, or being tardy too many times.

Every scenario will not be as vastly different as a dream vacation versus going to work, but for some people they need the extra push to get out of bed each day. It brings me to think about people I know with children. More often than not, they will tell you when they are at their lowest point in life, it is the idea of giving their children a better life that keeps them going each day. Even that is an external motivator. It's not something internal that gives them strength, but an outside force.

Sometimes an external motivator is needed until you can figure out how to grow the internal motivation. I often hear this term interchanged with passion. Don't think you have to know what your passion is today. A lot of time passion comes from trial and error, working through ideas and finding out what you don't like. Some people are very blessed to have found their passion early, and those are the highlights we see often.

Think of professional athletes and celebrities. Not all of them reached their pinnacle in the earlier stages of life. The main thing they all have in common is they worked through opportunities, found and believed in themselves. Do you believe in yourself? You have to believe you are great before anyone else can. In this instance, you have to find that internal motivation or even self-esteem before anyone else can feel your passion.

Consistency breeds motivation. When you are in motion, it's easier to stay in motion. When I get stuck with either writing or painting, I stay in motion, but move in a different direction. So if I am painting and working on a technique that I find especially difficult; I won't stop altogether. What I will do is move on to something else. Instead of painting and frustrating myself, I will sketch, or I will work on a different piece, or I may even sit down and watch videos about the technique I am working to master. I am indirectly working on my deficit while building my confidence to go back in and work on that technique.

The point is, I have a motivation to learn and finish it. That motivation is external because it is a commissioned piece that I will be paid for. That motivation is also internal because it is a piece for *me* that I have learned something new and grown in my craft. Being consistent helps keep me motivated. I find it harder to start from the beginning than to just keep going.

That makes me think of conversations with runners. I have always heard the hardest thing you can do as a runner is stop, walk and start running again. If you keep running, even just by slowing down, you eventually hit "the wall" and find a second wind. Your mind gives up before your body does. Let me say that again, your *mind* gives up before your body does. That relates to everything we think and do.

With motivation, your mind will talk you out of doing so much. It could range from wearing a particular outfit, to applying for your dream job, or moving to a new place, or going out to dinner by yourself. The examples are endless, but our mind will only produce what we put there. Jim Rohn once said, *"The mind is like a garden, it will produce whatever seeds you plant."* What are you plating in your mind? What is hindering you from reaching your next level? What is stopping you from being utterly impressed with yourself every day?

Sometimes our thoughts keep us from progress. If we let it stay in our heads, we give it power. We are going to release those thoughts today. We are going to till the soil of our mental gardens so we can plant new, healthy seeds. In the space below, list the defeating thoughts you may have. Thoughts of doubt, what someone else may think or say about your decisions, comparative thoughts that leave you feeling worse not better. List them below or on a separate sheet of paper.

My defeating thoughts are:

____

____

____

____

____

____

____

____

____

That exercise was not to upset or trigger you. It was created to allow you to get the thoughts *out* of your head, so they won't be distractions anymore. I want you to take that page and tear it out. If you wrote on a separate sheet of paper, great. Now, you are going to either burn it, shred/cut it, or rip it up and throw it away. As you do this, I want you to repeat, *"I am stronger than my thoughts, I control my mind and my actions."* Repeat this louder and louder until you believe it, until it has become truth to you. Release those feelings of doubt into the pages that you are physically trashing. Now shake it off. Commit to this being a daily practice.

Let's talk more about your W.H.Y. Since we have tilled our soil, we need to find some new seeds. Do you remember those 5-7 goals in the #GetToKnowYou exercise? For those goals, I want you to list why they are either going to help you or what about them hurts you enough to make you want to accomplish them. I think about it from an internal perspective.

What is it about those goals that makes you want to finish them? If its weight loss; examples are *I will lose weight, so I feel more confident. I will lose weight, so my clothes fit in a way that makes me feel comfortable.* If a goal is to get a promotion; examples are *I am working towards a promotion, so I can recognize my growth in my career. I am working towards a promotion so I can generate more income to travel more.* I have provided a few examples, yours don't have to look like this.

1. ____

2. ____

3. ____

4. ____

5. ____

6. ____

7. ____

These lines are now the start to a strong W.H.Y. Looking back at these will help you on days you don't feel so motivated. Just as the Zig Ziglar quote says, motivation does wear off, so we recommend it daily. Knowing how important it is to you can help you actualize those thoughts and wants. When you manifest them, you start to feel differently about yourself, your confidence goes up and you add more to your list. Results become, dare I say, addicting.

This makes me think of my own journey, my own defeating thoughts and my own W.H.Y. which turned into me starting my mobile paint studio. Guess what time it is, **Story Time**!

Spring of 2017, I was fighting a health battle and was losing pretty badly. I was diagnosed with jaundice and toxic liver. I rarely wanted to leave the house except for work. And even then, it was straight home to make sure no one saw me. I became a recluse. As I searched for ways to heal myself and overcome what couldn't be explained, my mother tried to get me involved in some excitement. Every suggestion she had, I turned down or cancelled.

One afternoon she suggested we attend a public paint event at a local restaurant. Hesitant, I agreed with all plans of cancelling at the last minute. It was nearing her birthday so that was her saving grace. That event, the normally extroverted and lively Candace, sat quietly and painted her picture. It was a sea turtle, appropriate as that's my mother's favorite animal, but all I wanted to do was melt into the floor.

There were pictures being taken from every angle for company marketing. I would turn my head, thinking, "I'm going to look like a jack o' lantern in each of these shots." I followed the instructions and kept quiet as to not bring too much attention to myself or our table. I was more fixated on what people thought of me than enjoying my time with my mother and the painting itself. Finally, because there was no way around it in the two-hour session, I let myself go and dived into the painting. It was the first time in weeks, I felt like I was in control of something.

While creating this sea creature, all I could hear in my head was, "just keep swimming." That day, while painting I made a decision that I wasn't going to let jaundice stop me from being who I am. Painting at that event triggered a sense of peace and confidence I hadn't felt in a long while, and I want to continue making sure that other people can overcome their mental blocks too. While I had enjoyed art before that moment; that day I became an artist and realized no matter *what*, my life is a masterpiece!

From that point, I spoke to the owner of the company and asked if they were hiring for any additional staff members. She said they were and encouraged me to apply. I submitted an application and early that summer I started as an assistant helping out at different paint parties around town. By this point, my illness had begun to clear up and I started feeling less self-aware.

I am still convinced it was due to me finding a new focus and staying in motion instead of sitting around thinking about how this illness was taking over my life. I enjoyed each event I assisted with, meeting people, making some extra money, but most importantly I felt I was making a difference by showing people how they too, through art, could find peace. This went on all summer, and by early fall we had a team meeting where we were told they were selling the company and we would be disbanded.

That day, I felt a punch to my stomach because this had become my outlet. Attending these events each week had become my motivation to get up and get out of the house. It wasn't about the money like my job was, it was about the feeling I got inside. I researched and offered to buy the company, a bold move seeing as how my capital was extremely low. I didn't know how I would do it; I just knew why I needed to do it. I needed to keep that outlet, I needed to keep creating and building with people. My purchase request was denied and that was the end of my artist career, or so I thought.

Fast forward a few months. It's now early November, I changed jobs and was working a commission only position that wasn't going so well. I was on the brink of my car being repossessed, and no sign of leaving my parents' house anytime soon. I again was feeling pretty low. Those defeating thoughts started creeping in again, mostly because my W.H.Y. was gone, and so was my internal motivation.

A friend's birthday was quickly approaching, and I couldn't afford to buy anything, but wanted to do something special as she was very supportive through my illnesses and surgeries. I had a few leftover canvases and paints and decided to throw her a mini paint party at my parents' house. We set it up outside, hoping the weather would stay nice enough to paint through. There were less than ten guests, so it was very intimate. I chose a piece of art that I had never painted before, but I allowed my love of the art and confidence in what art can do for you, to allow me to teach the painting.

We painted, we talked and all of a sudden, these different ideas and "life lessons" started streaming from me as I instructed. Nothing I was ever taught to do with the previous company, it was as if God was speaking directly through me to the artists at the table. There were cheers, and head nods of agreement and I started feeling more and more confident as each stroke crossed the canvas. We took some pictures and videos during our session and posted them to social media and from there within two weeks, I had booked another party. The irony being, it was never posted to be promotional for a business. That day, I mentally started *Canvases With Candace*, and didn't even realize it.

I had more than enough reasons to not start this business. No working capital, nowhere to borrow it from. I had since had my car repossessed, so mobile with no vehicle. No supplies, but I had clients. I could have let those obstacles, those defeating thoughts of "how are you going to pull this off," stop me; but I didn't. I was scared and unsure, but I knew what I had to offer was needed. My journey took a few turns down the road of motivation. It started externally, with going to the event with my mom. Transitioned to internal, because I needed the fulfillment art provided me. Then became external again, so I could gift my friend something for her birthday.

Finally, crossing back over into internal because it was something that gave me so much joy and I found a passion for it. In this moment, I didn't need any other validation than what I was giving myself. I wasn't sure just how far the business could or would grow, I hadn't thought that far in advance. What I did know was that I had a desire or intention, and now I can put the action towards it and wait for the results. I was motivated to see what the outcome could be. It was the idea of possibilities that gave me reinforcement to keep going. That was nearly two years ago, and the business has been exponentially growing ever since its inception.

As you can see from my story, external motivation can get you started, but internal motivation will keep you going.

#WhoseOpinionCounts

"Don't let the noise of others' opinions drown out your own inner voice."

-Steve Jobs

We have completed a self-assessment, evaluated our commitments and examined where motivation starts for us. With unlayering those concepts it brings us to our opinion of self, and how we feel other people view us. Have you ever had an idea, shared it with someone and their response was either, "Well I think you should just..." or, "Well I don't know why you would..."? How about, "In my opinion, I think..." Do any of these opening statements sound familiar to you? Yeah, they do to me too.

Take a moment and think about the last year. In that year, how many opinions do you think you've received about *you.* How many "observations" have been offered that weren't requested? Now think about how you responded to those opinions. Did you change your behavior due to those opinions? Did you ignore them and continue on your path? Did those opinions cause you to rethink your next steps? We've all fell prey to the "concerned friend/family member" who offered an opinion that wasn't solicited or warranted for that matter. What we *do* with that opinion is what makes the difference.

By definition, opinion is a noun that means "a belief or judgement that rests on grounds insufficient to produce complete certainty." We of course, are all guilty of offering our opinions as well. Usually, an opinion follows an action or statement we do not agree with. We as a people have a compelling urge to tell someone our thoughts regarding a situation without permission or invitation.

Can you think of three people whose opinion matters to you? Write them here.

I value the opinion of:

1. ____

2. ____

3. ____

Why do you value their opinion? Is it because they give sound advice? Is it because they have a lifestyle or experience that you desire? Would you consider them an "expert" in any one particular subject? Does their opinion typically mirror or validate your thoughts or situation?

Let's try this. Take a moment and think about yourself. For just a moment, erase the names from your mind and descriptions they may use to identify you. For this entry, I want you to spend some time defining yourself by *your* standards. Use the space below to describe yourself without using physical descriptions or titles. How would you introduce yourself if you weren't yourself? Would you say you are a caring person? A loud person? A humorous person? Be as specific as you can.

As you look over the words you've used to describe yourself, were they more negative or positive? Would you say you have high or low self-esteem? Did you find that exercise to be difficult or rather easy?

Here are two columns. With thinking about how you view yourself which words do you think best describe you?

Circle one in each row:

High Self-Esteem	Low Self-Esteem
Positive	Negative
Easy	Difficult
Confident	Doubtful
Courageous	Fearful

Did you have more circles on the left or right side? If there were more circles on the right, you are taking good steps to continue that perspective. If you have more circles in the right column, don't worry, you are in the right place to start changing how you view yourself into someone you can be impressed with.

Oftentimes, we rely on relationships for our identity; our friendships, romantic partners, family and co-workers. Who are we without these attachments? While our attachments and relationships are important to us, we cannot allow them to define us. We must stop relying on their descriptions of us and stop trying to fit into the box they have built. Oftentimes, you can find yourself stressed out for reasons unknown because you are trying to fit into this box that is probably too small.

If someone doesn't have a vision for themselves, how are they supposed to have a vision for you? It's very easy to tell someone else what they should be doing when you are on the outside looking in. When taking "advice" from someone, the first question I ask myself is, "Does this person have the intended results I want from the potential advice they are going to give me?" If I can't answer that question with a resounding yes, I decline to ask them.

For example, would you go to your doctor and ask for plumbing advice? Of course not, if you want plumbing advice, you'll go to a plumber. So why ask your single friend for relationship advice? You are both in the same boat and their experiences, while valid, are only going to get you as far as they have gotten. You must seek from a person with a higher experiential threshold. Now, of course there are exceptions to every rule, but we aren't talking about the exceptions here.

Some people will have a problem for every solution and if you continue to surround yourself with those types of people, their opinion will always outweigh yours. Why? Negativity is a very powerful force if you are not strong in your positivity. You have to be so rooted in the investment in your happiness and positivity that you can't be shaken with an opinion. Your opinion about yourself and your decisions should always be stronger than anyone else's. Allow those opinions to be "buffet style," take what you need from it and leave the rest. This I have found to be very helpful and allowed me to tailor my interactions with those who have limiting belief systems because mine are so strong.

There are so many people who will try and discourage you from things due to their own fears. You could want to move to a new state. If you ask someone who has never left their hometown, they may tell you all the reasons why it's a terrible idea. They may try to instill doubt and fear into your decision. On the other hand, someone who has traveled; experienced other places and cultures, while they may not agree with you leaving, they can give a more objective assessment of your decision and help you work through it to make an actual plan.

You may want to go back to school. Asking someone who doesn't value formal education may not be the person you want to talk to, as their opinion will be biased. Asking someone who has gone to school, (regardless if they enjoyed it or are benefitting from it) may have a more rational response. They may be better equipped to talk you through the process and see if that is what you truly desire to do. Either way, you should always feel confident enough in your opinion to have the final say.

This brings me to ask about your circle. Who do you consider your tribe? What types of people are they? This circle can directly shape how you form your opinion not just of yourself, but of things around you. Having healthy relationships is a very important part of living a life you can be impressed with. Not only are those friends a reflection of you, but you are also a reflection of them. Jim Rohn says, "You are the sum of the five people you spend the most time with." Well, think about that, is it true for you? I think of relationships in layers.

Your **Inner Circle**, **Middle Circle** and **Outer Circle.**

Inner Circle (IC)

- Close to you

- Understands you

- You trust them to be there for you

- Small number of people

- Can be vulnerable with them

- Strong influence on each other

- Greatly impact how you feel about yourself

You make a high level of emotional investment into this group. If you let too many people into your inner circle you can start to feel used, confused, heartbroken and drained as you usually spend most of your energy on those in this circle. This group is usually made of siblings, best friends, romantic partners and family members.

Middle Circle (MC)

- You enjoy spending frequent time with them

- Share experiences

- Have common interests

- Much larger number of people

- Reliable, but not typically who you put a lot of trust in

You don't make as much of an emotional investment in this group. You will share opinions and experiences, but not usually your innermost thoughts, feelings and dreams. These relationships are usually fluid and can be stronger or weaker depending on where you are in life, your current interests and hobbies as well as the time you spend together. These people can usually be your close co-workers, people apart of common clubs or social groups and close neighbors.

Outer Circle (OC)

- You have regular or infrequent contact with them

- Usually conversations are small talk

- The connections are not deep

- Very large number of people

- Share quick and short experiences with

- No real level of trust

You don't make much if any emotional investment into this group of people. This group usually consists of distant old or current classmates, co-workers, community members, neighbors, church members and social media contacts. These relationships are very fluid and change frequently. Loss of contact does not typically affect you, as they are often only short spans of time for connections.

Fill in the circles below:

Now that you have completed your circles, consider these five questions:

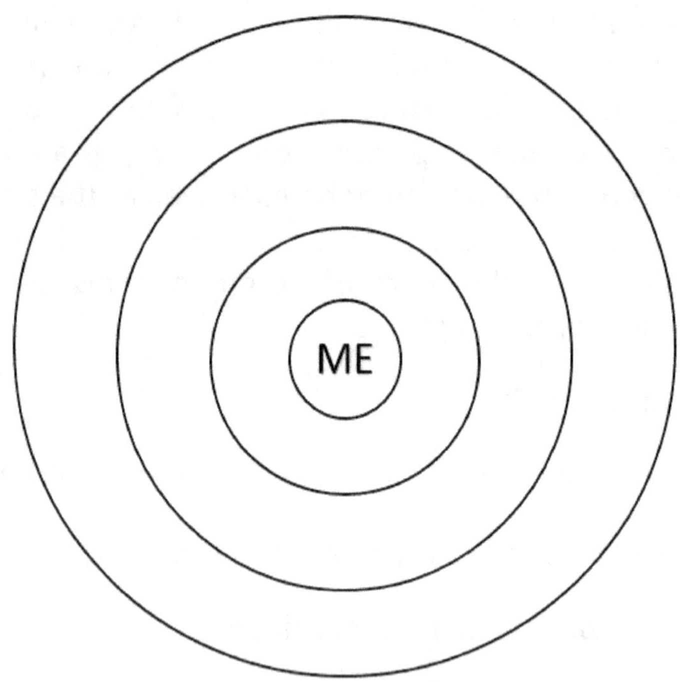

1.   What are three things you should/would talk about only to those in your IC?

____

____

____

____

2.   Have you ever regretted sharing something with your MC or OC?

____

____

____

____

3.   Does a person's age/gender impact where they are in your three circles?

____

____

____

____

4.   Is someone in your MC or OC that you want to be closer to? Is there anyone in your IC that you want to move to your OC?

____

____

____

____

5.   How emotionally affected are you by the opinions (positive or negative) of those in your **IC**? **MC**? **OC**?

____

____

____

____

Let's talk about these answers. I believe you should have those you can share your innermost thoughts with and feel safe when you do. Not just people who will always agree with you, but people who know and understand you. They are able to give you advice not just opinions. They can help map out ideas and create plans for those ideas and feelings. You may take their advice, you may not. However, you know they are speaking out of love, care and concern. They aren't projecting their insecurities and fears on you. Keep these people close.

If you have regretted sharing intimate processes with those in your MC or OC, it's ok. Hopefully it is something you learned from and are able to start to compartmentalize those people and find better ways to share those thoughts/ideas with those in your IC. The one thing I would challenge you to consider is why you felt compelled to share with them and what was it about the exchange that made you regret sharing? Also, did you share this same information with your IC, and how did they respond in comparison?

What factors do you consider when you allow someone into either of these three circles? If age or gender does play a part, I urge you to consider why. Whatever preference you have for those in your circles is completely your decision. Whoever you choose is up to you. Do you see any patterns of the types of people in your circles?

There are times when people get moved from one circle to the other. Be sure you are creating a toll for that. Require specific criteria when it comes to your IC. Be intentional in who you have closest to you. Some people can earn their way from outer rungs as time goes on. Only you know what that rubric is, make it and stick to it. As you evolve, that level of measurement should evolve too.

It is not uncommon for the opinions of those in our IC to affect us the most, as they should compared to our MC or OC; not necessarily to ourselves. We give them the most energy and trust. We are the most vulnerable with them and expect them to handle us with the utmost care. Have you ever had someone in your IC give you a harsh opinion while someone in your MC or OC gave you compliments or encouragement? That can sometimes give you a false sense of deeper connection and closeness. Again, be mindful of who you are receiving opinions from. Those in your MC and OC may not know you well enough to give an honest opinion.

It can be the case that those closest to us, are so close they can't see the vision you see. They are creating their opinion based on everything they know about you holistically versus the current situation as an isolated circumstance. Remember these are the people who have seen you at your best and worst. More often than not, they are trying to protect you not only from outside forces, but sometimes from yourself too.

For example, you want to start at a new gym with a personal trainer. You mention it to your MC/OC and they give you encouragement, ask for details and the conversation stays pretty surface because they only know you well enough to take your word as it stands. You mention it to someone in your IC and they ask deeper questions or even scoff at you because they have seen you join numerous gyms and quit, numerous programs and fall off and follow several fads before dwindling away.

I am not suggesting you stop talking to your IC if they don't agree with decisions or give you a hard time with their opinion. They may be trying to protect you from beating yourself up if you quit even if you don't anticipate it. Or, they could be trying to save you from disappointment later if you aren't getting the results you want because they aren't used to seeing you do the work you said you would do. I am encouraging you to do some self-reflection as well to see how true the opinion is based on how you feel about yourself. If you agree with the opinion, it is usually harder to shake off the negative comments. If you disagree with the opinion, stand firm in your decisions. Even if you decide to quit again, don't allow the opinion to be the reason you did. Make your decisions for the innermost circle on your chart, *you!*

This reminds me of a story. Guess what? It's **Story Time**!

Most of my life I have been known for having lengthy, thick, healthy hair. I'd always been the girl to wear it in a ponytail or a wrap for the most part. (If you don't know what a wrap is do an internet search for wrap hairstyle). I always felt it was one of my best physical attributes. Due to it being so dark and shiny, I had always refused suggestions to add color or highlights, for fear of damage as it was processed as well. I believed the slicker the ponytail the better. I stopped processing my hair for a year and a half. I grew it out and kept it in braids for most of that time. Finally, after 31 years of refusal, I finally broke down and colored part of my hair with a peek-a-boo honey brown color. It was still black until you brushed it a certain way. It took me out of my comfort zone, but I loved it. I received so many compliments on it, it really made me feel great about my decision.

A few months later, after losing my job, and what I am convinced was stress related, my hair started shedding and falling out rapidly. Within a few weeks my thick ponytail looked like a tattered wig in need of new strands and some tlc. I had patches and plugs missing from my scalp. Every time I shampooed my hair it was coming out in clumps. I was devastated. I tried new moisturizers, new shampoo and conditioner, new hair care routines; nothing was working. I was noticing it and other people were too. I didn't get the compliments I once did and I always felt a need to mention to those who knew me, "I think it's breaking off from that color, see this is why I never wanted to color it before." While the color may have played a part, I'm sure it was much more than that.

I talked it over with my partner at the time that I was considering cutting all my hair off. After a few discussions, I decided to get an undercut to where I would still have the hair on the top and middle part of my head, but everything from my ears and down would be cut into a design. As the person who affectionately has been called, "Sampson" from the Biblical story, (he was the man who never cut his hair because it was the source of his superhuman strength from God), I finally decided to go to the barber shop and cut my hair.

I sat there unfazed, ready to try something new. The cut was over, and I was pleased with it. I got home and proudly showed off my new style, only for my partner to respond apathetically. It stung a little. Mostly because I was sensitive about having to cut it to begin with and I expected a much better response. I felt self-conscious for a day or two, and decided it wasn't exactly the look I was going for. Now it was cut and there was no way to reverse it. It didn't really change what was happening to my hair. It gave it a new look, but it was still damaged.

I slept on it and decided exactly one week later to just go to the shop and cut it all off. I was going to do the big chop! I didn't tell my partner this time, because I didn't want to discuss it and I didn't want to be talked out of it. I shampooed it one last time, let it air dry. As it dried my hair strands swelled, creating a poof that strongly resembled a lion's mane. I remember a calm sense of strength the day I sat back in the barber's chair. I walked back in and said, "Just cut it all." I leaned back with the cape around me and closed my eyes as I felt the cool buzz of the clippers against my scalp. At that moment I exhaled and released my negative feelings into the hair falling to the floor.

That haircut took some time as I kept asking the barber to go lower. I took progression pictures during the process, and with each click of the camera shutter I felt more and more confident in my decision. I felt more confident because I didn't seek permission or opinions from anyone before I did it, I just did it. It was for me and no one else, so why did it matter what they had to say? When we finally finished, I rubbed my nearly bald head and couldn't do anything but smile. I did it and it was done. I walked out of the shop with my chin up and the sun hitting the back of my neck and it felt *great!*

One of the first people to see my new lack of hair was my mother, who also took pride in my and my sister's hair. The first thing she said when she saw me was, "What did you *do?* You cut *all* your hair *off?*" She was not pleased and was probably in a slight state of shock. I proudly stood there, rubbed my head, and said what I already knew the answer to be, "Yeah, you like it?" with the biggest smile on my face. "No, I don't like it," she yelled. "Now you really look like a boy, why would you do that?"

I had already braced my emotional self for that response, so I wasn't as affected as I would have been the week before. I straightened my back, pulled my shoulders back and responded, respectfully, "I wanted to and needed to. It was damaged and I need it to grow back healthy, no sense on keeping it if it's not growing the right way." The conversation went on for a few and we parted ways, but for the first time in a long time someone in my inner circle was able to give me an opinion I didn't agree with, but I also. didn't feel emotionally attacked. I felt proud of my decision and was able to stand firm in it. In that moment, the *only* opinion that mattered was mine.

You may be thinking, well this was just a story about getting a haircut for the first time, but for me it was so much more. My hair had been so much of my identity from childhood. I was known as the girl who had such nice hair for a brown skinned girl. It was often compared to my sister's hair which was just as long, if not longer, but more manageable. This is not just a story of a haircut, but of learning to cut off the opinions of others; even if at one point it was what I looked to for validation. I learned to find validation in my *own* feelings and opinions about myself.

Now three years later, my hair is just about the length it was before, I still get the same compliments, but about my natural hair. The curl pattern, the waves, how dark and shiny it is, just as I did before. However, this time, I have already said those things to myself about 10 times before I even left the house. Those opinions are now highlights to my day, versus the main attraction. I am able to take those compliments without my feeling of self-worth changing.

#FailureIsNotForever

"Everything that exists in your life, does so because of two things: something you did or something you didn't do."

-Albert Einstein

Failure by definition is a noun, meaning, an act or instance of failing or proving unsuccessful. However, nowhere in this definition does it say failure is lasting or permanent. At some point in your life, you lived without a fear of failure. You lived with no understanding of what failure feels like. You don't believe me, do you? I bet you don't remember learning how to walk. Have you seen a toddler lately? Watching them go through the process of standing up, holding on to something, taking a few steps and then BOOM they hit the floor. They may be startled. They may pause and regain their bearings, but guess what else they do? They get back up and do it again.

They fall, get back up and do it again tirelessly until one day, they start walking. You did the same thing. You failed over and over again until, one day you just got it. The reason is because you never stopped. You didn't allow the failure in the moment to hinder you from getting to the intended goal. A baby doesn't look around and analyze who saw them fall, and now they won't make an attempt in front of that person again. Babies don't know what embarrassment is. They will keep going until it happens.

What is the difference between you today and you learning how to walk back then? As we grow, we begin to have experiences, these experiences tend to shape how we continue in situations. What do you do with the things you aren't afraid of? You just do them. You make a decision, whether you realize it or not, to just get it done. I'm not saying we aren't allowed to be cautious, or skeptical about things. I'm not saying we shouldn't think things through and weigh the pros and cons of our decisions. What I am saying is we have moments of fear and processing, but don't allow those moments to stop and inhibit you from moving forward. I remember watching a movie and hearing Will Smith's character say, *"Danger is real, fear is a choice."* That quote resonated with me. It sparked a moment for me to evaluate things I was irrationally fearful of. This quote pops into my mind when I am trying something new; it could be food, a new environment, or even meeting a new person. I have fears and doubts that will swirl through my mind, but the quote brings me back to earth, reminding me there is nothing to fear.

Let's try this, list the last attempt you made that you considered yourself to have failed at. What was the action, the anticipated result and what happened for you to consider it a failure?

____

____

____

____

____

When you think of this moment, who pointed out it was a failure? Was it the reaction of other people? Was it an internal disappointment? Were you comparing your result to that of someone else? Did you feel embarrassed for not completing the action, or not getting your intended results?

I believe embarrassment or self-doubt stems from relying too much on other's opinions to validate what we set out to accomplish. That is one factor. Sometimes we do things because they are expected of us, not because we really want to do them. The other factor being we didn't really believe we could accomplish what we set out to do; there was no internal **WHY**. Remember we must have a reason to get into action. Validation can be the reason and is a normal pseudo-emotion. As we have discussed before, *where* you get the validation from becomes the important key factor. What is it going to take for *you* to believe in yourself?

There is a saying about failure being a test to how bad you want something. Can you keep pushing to get to the result? Conversely, there is another saying, that instructs us to know when to give up. That's pretty confusing, right? Do I keep going or should I stop? How do I know? There is no rule book to it.

This Catch-22 has given me *many* sleepless nights in my own pursuit of goals and aspirations. Through my experiences, I have come to the conclusion that both are right. Anytime you want something, and you want it bad, it may not be the easiest to obtain. Think about the baby. We didn't say the baby stood up once and took steps and never fell again. There was a series of attempts, reworking the strategy and finally reaching the desired result.

Making a decision to stop working towards a specific goal doesn't make you a failure. You could have lost interest, like we discussed with motivation and intentions. You could be distracted, not giving your full energy to the matter. Through reworking the strategy, you could realize your initial plan wasn't well thought out. It could be a matter of pausing in pursuit of this goal and shifting gears to another goal. Have you ever seen the memes and stories about some of the most "famous failures?"

Example, Michael Jordan. Widely known as one of, if not the greatest, basketball players of all time. MJ was cut from his high school basketball team. What he didn't do was give up. Was he upset? I'm sure he was. However, as we can see, he took that energy and used it to fuel himself to get better.

Oprah is one of the richest, most successful women in the world. She created her empire from broadcast television but was fired from her first news anchor job. She could have looked at that situation as a failure, and decided she was giving up. However, she didn't, when they closed the door on her, she built her own.

We don't necessarily know what they felt internally, but whatever it was, it didn't pull them back. It propelled them forward. The image I'm seeing in my head now is a bow and arrow. You pull it back, and it builds up tension. Once you release just one finger, the arrow is shot in the direction it's pointed. The pressure that is built behind the arrow will determine just how far it will go. When we fail, we're like that arrow. We are temporarily pulled back. We can feel the pressure. We have to aim ourselves in the right direction; and *use* the pressure to catapult us forward.

Failure is truly a part of life. It's inevitable, no matter who you are. This is why I don't think it is failure we are really afraid of. It's rejection. It's the pain and discomfort of feeling dismissed or unworthy. This can cause a loss in resiliency which is too often translated into a fear of failure. The anticipation of rejection hinders a genuine pursuit of what you truly desire. It's seemingly easier to talk about what you *thought* about doing, than to discuss how you attempted and failed. The thing about it is if you never work towards something you still failed, because you removed your option to succeed.

Think back to elementary science class, we all learned the same thing about experiments. You have an idea, create a hypothesis and then test it. Either the hypothesis was true or false. We weren't taught the experiment was a failure we were taught to create a new hypothesis and retest. We ruled out false hypotheses until we were able to have enough information to yield a conclusion.

Let's look back at your last identified failure. First, we are going to change our language from failure to "unfinished." Let's pinpoint where the breakdown happened for you.

What were the obstacles that hindered you from completing it?

____

____

____

____

What mistakes did you make, that if you could go back, you would do differently?

____

____

____

____

Is there anything stopping you from restarting or approaching it?

____

____

____

____

Are you in the same mental space now as you were when you left it unfinished?

____

____

____

____

Did you have a **WHY** when you started on it the first or second time?

____

____

____

____

What was your **WHY** then? If you did not have a **WHY** then, do you have one now?

____

____

____

____

I'd like us to work together to make a three-step action plan to take this off the shelf, or pick something else altogether, and refocus your energy. By answering the previous questions, we can determine if your choice is aligned with where you are going in life or if you need to separate from it. At times, we must separate to elevate. Someone once gave me advice, "Stop recycling what should be replaced." It is okay to let it go if it is no longer serving you; make room for better.

Step 1: Identify if the action/thing is still a desire. First you must determine if you in fact _want_ to finish or accomplish this thing. Looking at your previous answers, identify what the purpose is. Is it something to elevate you personally? Financially? Emotionally? Physically? Spiritually? Have you grown into or out of the person you need to be to finish it?

Step 2: Identify why you are afraid of it. What is really holding you hostage? Has someone discouraged you? Has someone already completed what you are wanting to do? Here is a word of advice, if its been done once, _you_ can do it too! Finding out why you are truly fearful will help you identify the root of the issue and tackle that first. If you can change the mentality about being afraid, that can change your energy towards it as well.

Step 3: Learn from your mistakes and go for it again. Every disappointment is an opportunity to grow, learn and gain experience. You can get back to working towards "it" making sure to stay away from your own previous pitfalls. Every step you take towards the end result, you will gain more and more experience. This experience will also prepare and build your confidence for other projects and ideas as well.

Did you realize a rubber band is a very resilient object? It can be stretched over and over again based on it's make up. We are very similar to rubber bands in the way that we too can be stretched, and while uncomfortable it can be done. You got this!

Accountability is another huge factor in why we could be fearful of leaving something "unfinished." I have accountability partners for a few areas of my life. Having one is helpful because it's someone I can trust, someone who has either gone through or is going through the same process I am. They are able to ask me questions to keep me on track as well as offer gentle reminders and guidance through the process. So, let's talk about this idea of accountability. When you are working through your process in any area of life how do you hold yourself accountable? Do you keep a journal of your progress? Do you set calendar reminders to complete things? Reminders using your smartphone? A person who checks in with you at increments?

I like to use a combination of all these things. Often, I'm able to stay on task, but there are moments when I need to be reeled back in and refocused. Have you ever felt like that? I love using "to do" lists. They help me organize my thoughts and give me a sense of accomplishment when I am able to check things off. Usually, I will start with a high-level idea/goal and then break it down into each task it will take to complete it. So, it would look something like this:

Bedroom closet

- Separate shirts from pants
- Organize by style
- Organize by color
- Remove clothes I can no longer fit
- Separate work clothes from casual clothes

Linen closet

- Towels
- Washcloths
- Sheet sets
- Blankets

That may seem like a simple example, but to just have "Reorganize closets" on my list leaves me too much time to either get off task or get stuck in what I really want to complete. I also like to entertain my "but, can't we..." (BCDubs) Your "BCDubs" is that little voice in your head that wants to distract you. Like when cleaning out the closets, it's the little voice saying "but, can't we try this on," or "ooh but can't we watch that Netflix show, you should watch it now instead of cleaning out this closet." See your "BCDubs" likes to play, and frolic, and not get any work done. Your "BCDubs" is responsible for your mindless scrolling on social media. Oh, come on, we have all done it.

Your "BCDubs" is only motivated by one thing; distracting you. It will often need an incentive to get something done. What I do to incentivize my BCDubs? I set time limits on things, and then give BCDubs what it wants. *Only,* once we have finished in the time frame. Like with the closets; if I give myself a time limit of one hour to separate the shirts from pants, organized by style and color, separate work from casual, and remove clothes I can't fit or wear and my BCDubs *helps*, (or at least doesn't distract me) during that hour, *then* we get to do something more entertaining.

It may not be in that exact moment, but I give my BCDubs a treat for being helpful. It may be that we can go to the movies on Friday; or we can go out for ice cream later that day. Incentivizing myself is really helpful in getting things done. Now the hard part is *not* giving yourself, I mean your BCDubs, the incentive if you haven't finished.

We have free will. We can do what we want, we just have to want to do it. Usually it is the glamorous stuff we like to do, and the gopher or grunt work we don't want to. Conversely, if things start to get too bad, and I'm behind on a deadline I've set for myself; I will implement a "punishment." That can sometimes be as simple as unplugging my T.V. for a few days until I get through with what I set out to do. My BCDubs is notorious for wanting to scroll social media mindlessly, so sometimes that punishment is putting my phone in a completely different room while I work. This eliminates the distraction and causes me to have to get up and physically move to become distracted. Please do not confuse this with the general idea of taking a break from a task. These are just a few ways I hold myself accountable in the moment, for short term things.

Do you have any things you do to reward your BCDubs? What are a few things you could use as incentives? Some examples could be buying a new shirt, watching your favorite show or taking a nap.

Incentives:

____

____

____

____

____

What about restrictions? What are some things you could take away for a short time to get your BCDubs to get to work? Examples could be removing your phone, no T.V., no favorite snacks.

____

____

____

____

____

____

By implementing these ideas, I have been able to start accomplishing so much more on a daily basis. I needed that in my life at one point. I had become so overwhelmed with not knowing how to break down and accomplish my big ideas. This has really helped me drastically reduce my "to do" list and grow my "done" list.

Another thing about failure is it's something we all will experience at some point, but it also means we are *doing* something. Think about it, it is impossible to fail if you are *doing* nothing. We must fail in order to grow and learn. We have all began learning something and stumbled through it. I can remember learning to play the clarinet when I was in middle school. I was bad at first; no bad is an understatement, I was terrible.

You could hear the loudest screeches coming from my room, which typically meant I had cracked yet another reed. I could have been discouraged by comparing myself to my classmates who were learning much faster than me. For a little while, I did become discouraged. I slowly stopped practicing as much, conveniently leaving my instrument at school over weekends and breaks. Until one day my mom sat me down and asked if it was something I really wanted to do. I had to take a hard look at what I really wanted and if not being "good" was enough to make me quit. I decided to keep going. What I learned from that is not to limit myself based on what I didn't know, but to increase the time I spent learning. I went on to play the clarinet for another five years and eventually made it to first chair (that the best player in the section and is determined on an incremental basis).

What you must do in knowing you will fail at some things and knowing you will run into hurdles along the way is, be okay with getting uncomfortable. Change and growth will feel weird at times. Doing things in spite of what you *think* you can do, can be a very strange feeling. And this only gets harder as we get older. You become settled, comfortable where you are. Sometimes it's easier to *talk* about what you need to do, than to actually do it. One of my favorite quotes by motivational speaker Les Brown is, "If you do what is hard, life will be easy, if you do what is easy life will be hard."

Living in the land of "ok" is not a residence you want to reside in. The land of "ok" is the land of mediocrity, average, uninspired even. You are not uninspired. You are not average; you are not mediocre. So, take yourself out of that place. Pack your bags and take a journey to the land of phenomenal, outstanding and extraordinary.

Recognition is usually another factor when it comes to feeling like something was a failure. Recognition can come from different places and have different values to each of us. On your job, when you've done something above and beyond; it may feel pretty good to have your boss or coworkers recognize that. Most often we'd like the recognition in the form of a raise, right?! But no, seriously, it does feel good when someone can point out things we've done without our prompt. It validates our actions and can reinforce our behavior. Now we have to ask ourselves, what if you never get recognition for it? Will that make you stop doing something? Will it be enough to deter you from continuing to do great work? Well since we are talking about work, it may cause you to feel unvalued, start to look for a different job, or just show up and do the bare minimum every day. All three outcomes aren't the greatest outcome, are they? What is the last thing you were recognized for at:

Work:

____

____

____

Home:

____

____

____

Community:

____

____

____

How did you feel after receiving recognition?

____

____

____

What if you took that same feeling and applied it to you for self-recognition? What would that look like for you? What if you started doing more things just for the sheer satisfaction of knowing *you* did it? Do you already recognize yourself for things you have done? What do you do to recognize yourself?

____

____

Recognition is something I have enjoyed and sought after most of my life. I went through a period where I almost craved it, and I believe that was because I didn't feel so great about myself at the time. I didn't have high self-esteem, so I looked for validation elsewhere. It's **Story Time**!

In June 2012, I joined a network marketing company. I was in a transitional period financially and wanted to generate some extra income and the company, from what I could see, seemed like it was a lot of fun and lucrative. I quickly started making sales and gaining some recognition in my local area of New York. I was doing presentations weekly and people were buying from me and my team frequently. I had grown a sales team of over 30 people in about three months. They were doing well and continuing to make sales too.

Leaders with much higher ranks were contacting me, encouraging me to keep going, and offering support. I eventually moved my team and business back to South Carolina, where there wasn't much traction and growth happening yet. I made a decision that I was going to be the trailblazer who would put the city on the map for our company.

When I got here, I did over 50 presentations in less than three weeks, and as per my proven track record, I just *knew* I was going to close at least half of the sales. Boy was I wrong. In three weeks, I closed one sale. It was a blow to my ego more than anything, as this self-proclaimed, "awesome saleswoman." My sales team was rooting for me and it was difficult to hear the disappointment in their voice after each presentation, that I wasn't able to close the deal.

The encouraging calls from my leaders started to slow down. I was starting to panic a little that I couldn't do this alone in a new area. Even with the fear; I never stopped. I kept going, and within a few more weeks I started to make some traction again. My team was growing in a new area and the calls started to pick up. Other leaders from other teams were now contacting me and wanting to collaborate. I was back in a position to receive lots of recognition.

So many people not in our company would tell me, "That's never going to work, you're wasting your time." I would explain they just didn't understand, and that I was going to be a millionaire doing this one day. I was able to help a lot of teams start to grow in our area, not all of them mine, but it was growing the company reputation, so I was still excited. This continued for some time. I started winning awards, getting bonuses and receiving national company recognition. I was doing well in my sales job at work. Taking a domestic vacation nearly every month and international vacations quarterly.

I had reached the level of the company where I was awarded with a luxury car, as long as I maintained a certain amount of sales per month. I was 30 years old, driving my dream car, making the most money I'd ever made in my life and living my dream. My parents beamed with pride every time they saw me; my cousins would tease and call me, "rich cousin Candace" when we went for family functions.

Other leaders were reaching out to me, having me train their teams, everyone spoke about me with such admiration and esteem. I was on top of the world. At this point I had created the largest sales team in our city, and

I was the highest ranking and income earning person in the area. I felt like a celebrity, and I fed off the "high." I was at a point where absolutely nothing could shake me. When I offered my opportunity to people to either buy my service or join my sales team and they declined, I felt bad for *them* not for me and my team, because we were having a great time. Or so I thought.

Not everyone on my team was making the income they wanted, some weren't using the product as much as they wanted to, and my team started to dwindle. People started leaving the company. They weren't coming to the events as much; they would say they couldn't do what I was doing as far as presenting the information. Those same "doubters" from before started showing up more. Asking more questions and almost taunting, "You made your million dollars yet?"

I started getting frustrated and confused. As a result of a lot of my team leaving, there became a shift in my income as well. My income was a direct reflection of how many sales I had, as well as a percentage of my team. I wanted to help them reach their goals, I wanted to just do it for them if I could, and that wasn't enough. So, my team was declining, and on top of that I was let go from my job.

Panic started to set in. I didn't know how I was going to be able to maintain the life I was living publicly. In private, it was all falling apart. I felt like I was trying to keep up the walls of a crumbling building all by myself. From the outside, no one really knew what was happening financially, you know the highlight reel was all they could see. I dug deep and decided I would save my team myself; I was the first domino to start the team and I could do it again. But I couldn't, I wasn't. I was still being seen as this amazing speaker and trainer, but I felt I was training people how to do what I couldn't do anymore. I felt like a failure. I lost some notches in my ranking with the company, the financial backing for the luxury car (that I could NOT afford on my own), but mostly I lost my friends that I was in business with.

All of this was happening, and I was starting to feel more and more empty every day. I was measuring myself against people who started after me, making more progress than me. Until that point, I had finally felt that I was "important," I had a significance bigger than myself; and I was losing it. It felt like trying to hold sand in my hands in a windstorm. No one really knew what was happening, but I was embarrassed anyway. I've never had a strong poker face, so when asked, "How's business going," I would often feel frozen and respond with, "Oh yeah you know it's going pretty good." Even though I knew it wasn't. The "things," the accolades, the popularity had become something I thrived on. Even in all of it, I couldn't determine what was making me truly happy.

I slowly disappeared from the limelight. While our personal rankings are recognized in the company, they aren't discussed if you've "lost rank." People would reach out to me, asking how I was doing and why I wasn't at events. I felt naked, as if everyone knew. I felt as if they were all judging me. I felt they were asking because they wanted me to know they knew what was really going on. I hid. I tucked my tail between my legs and disappeared. I didn't want to face the losses; I didn't want to acknowledge the failure. I didn't want to ask for help to get back up. I got knocked down and I stayed there.

From that period, I have still stayed with the company. I have still kept up with information and updates, but I haven't sold anything for a few years now. I had to take a hard look at myself and ask, "Why do you want to do this?" My answer for the most part was the recognition. I really liked the products and the company overall, but mostly the recognition. Once that was gone, I needed to find within myself a deeper reason why recognition was important.

I took some time away and started to do some self-evaluations. From that time, the concepts in this book were born. I started to look at things for what I loved about them versus what I could gain from them. I started realizing I didn't need to always be recognized for what I was doing, because life is fluid. I learned not to be embarrassed when I didn't reach a goal I was publicly striving for. I took that time to learn that I could teach myself and someone else how to be okay with losing. And not even losing, but learning.

From that experience, I was able to learn so much about business, personal growth and eventually was able to start my own business. I was able to walk into my own business a few years later with a renewed mindset. A stronger inner and outer shell. I was able to learn, sometimes you have to leave something "unfinished" to begin a new journey. I have learned to not become overwhelmed with what I cannot control. I have learned that as long as I seek validation with myself, there is nothing I can't do. I have learned to stop wanting to have other people impressed with me and to be impressed with myself.

Now, I am able to talk to people about my experience without feeling embarrassed but empowered. I'm able to look at those same "doubters" in the face, and with confidence, tell them where I am in life. I no longer look at that time of my life as the, "I should have or could have done..." period. I see it as a time I was able to create some amazing memories, experiences and friends. I was able to grow and elevate my mind which put me in a position to now do the things I truly love doing, and do them for ME.

Now it's your turn. What has your last "big failure" taught you? What can you take from it to propel you forward? If you feel you are still in it, what can you identify right now to reassure yourself that there is something to learn from? What do you think you need, to release yourself from the bondage of failure?

#MeetMeAtTheFinishLine

"Victory is not won in miles, but in inches. Win a little now, hold your ground, and later win a little more."

-Louis L'Amour

We all set goals. We set goals everyday whether we realize it or not. A goal is simply a plan with a desired outcome. Your goals can be big or small, there is no rule that says otherwise. There are so many things we do daily and don't realize they are goals, or even milestones as a part of a larger goal. I like to think of goals as more of a finish line and those milestones are more like mile markers along the way. The mile markers are checkpoints to evaluate if you are on target to reach your finish line in the anticipated time frame.

I used to play basketball, and I would connect the finish line to winning the championship; the mile markers to each game. Each game gave our team and me the opportunity to learn our weaknesses, but also see our growth and improvements over time. Sometimes, we can spend so much time thinking about and focusing on the finish line, we forget to celebrate the mile markers. It can be very easy to think about how far you have to go; it's easy to forget how far we've come. Setting visual goals can help with this. When you can *see* what you've done it makes that finish line more tangible.

I'm sure you are currently setting goals, whether you realize it or not. What we are going to do is categorize these goals and make them a little easier for you to focus on. When you categorize the goals, you are able to set a plan for each, and recognize where you need the most help or where you are excelling the most as well. I'm going to give you my personal blueprint. I make no guarantees, but by using this blueprint I have been able to get "promoted" in my career, exponentially grow my business, generate more income, as well as write and publish a book.

So, what are goals anyway? Most think of goals as these life altering mountain moving concepts, that can take years to achieve. This is not exactly the case. While some goals can be lofty and take a bit more effort and time to complete, some can happen in a matter of hours, days, or weeks even. I think of these as more of the Short-Term Goals (STG). Those lofty ones can span across months, quarters and years, so I call these the Long-Term Goals (LTG). There is no real set number of how many goals you should have going on at the same time. Create goals based on what you can honestly handle, but don't be afraid to stretch yourself as well.

The heftiest goal type is the Lifetime Goal(s). These are goals that can take 10+ years to complete. Think of your overall future self, what do you see? Those things for the most part can be lifetime goals. Some of them will be attained by completing your STG and LTGs. Over time these goals may change. I'm sure we can all agree our goals at 15 were very different than age 25 onward. Every few years you may want to revisit your Lifetime Goals and readjust as necessary.

It can be easy to get overwhelmed with goals, but they are usually overwhelming if you don't have a clear and concise plan to complete them. I used to suffer from paralysis of analysis. I would spend so much time making the "perfect plan" that I wasn't working on the goal itself. When setting these goals, I want you to remember two main things. One, there will never be the "perfect time" to start working on anything, you just have to jump out and do it and adjust along the way. Two, don't underestimate what you can do in a year, and overestimate what you can do in 10.

When setting goals, you must have three main components:

1. What is the goal?

2. When will it be completed by?

3. Say it/Write it as if it already completed

Example: I have $100,000 saved in the bank on September 1, 2029.

This is an example of a lifetime goal; its set for 10 years from now, and it has all three components. When I speak of this goal, I can envision myself looking at my bank statement with $100,000 in it. Now will this money magically appear in my bank account; of course not. That would be nice wouldn't it? Ok I'm back. I have to set STG and LTGs to reach this. LTG could be to have $50,000 in the bank by September 1, 2024, that is the halfway point of five years from now. But where is this money coming from? Well that is where more STG and LTGs are coming from.

A STG could be to save 30% of all income revenues for the next year. That would mean from my job, and businesses. A way to check that goal is to take how much income comes in, subtract 30% and deposit into the bank monthly. Another STG would be to generate an additional stream of income. Another could be to bring lunch to work each week for two months and put what I would normally spend in the bank. That gives me a two-month goal as well as a one-year goal. At the end of that two months and one year I can check against my target to see if I am on track. If I am then I can keep the pace, if not I will need to reassess my current actions.

One thing that can hurt us when setting goals is not setting enough goals in different sections of life. We should have goals set in a variety of areas, not just financial. Here are a few categories:

- Financial
- Career/Business
- Personal/Educational
- Health/Wellness
- Spiritual/Mental Health

Setting goals in these areas can ensure you have a well-rounded life experience. Here are a few examples of goals in each of these areas:

Financial	Career/Business	Personal/Educational	Health/Wellness	Spiritual/Emotional Wellness
Savings	Promotion	Learn new language	Working out	Attending Church
Investments	Career Change	Reading more	Health checks	Praying
Decreasing Debt	Start a business	Become an expert in...	Increasing energy	Meditation
Large purchases	Get a specific award	Travel	Large fitness goal	Volunteer

You do not have to use these at all, but they are a few examples. Hopefully they have given you a few ideas of your own.

Setting the goal can be the easy part. Just writing it out and being able to visualize it. The fun, but sometimes daunting part, is tracking it. How do you track your goals now? I am a visual person so I like to use pictures and things I can see, check off or "fill in" to track my goals. If we keep to the theme of mile markers and finish lines, think of tracking it as your odometer, the gauge you use for each goal. If it's a money goal you could use a visual piggy bank and when you get to each level you fill it in until it's completely full. That may seem a bit elementary, but that can be a great way for you to recognize and reward yourself for reaching milestones.

Think back to our $100,000 goal. If that is broken up over 10 years, that's $10,000 per year. Every year by filling in that piggy bank you can *see* how close you are and what you've accomplished. There could be a reward for reaching each level each year, just make sure the reward doesn't take away from the goal. You reward yourself because you are reinforcing the positive behavior. Creating good habits can be hard and often draining. You are changing something you are used to doing and that should be acknowledged along the way.

When looking at health and wellness goals, a reward may be a new outfit or time at the spa. With career and business goals, a reward could be an office revitalization, or vacation. Add the reward to your goal, so now you have two things you are reaching for, the goal and the reward.

In my blueprint I use goal charts. Here is a filled in example of one:

Goal: I have 100,000 saved in the bank on September. 1, 2029

- ☐ Lifetime Goal
- ☐ Long Term Goal
- ☐ Short Term Goal

What steps do I need to take to have $100,000 in the bank on September 1, 2029

Long Term Steps

- ☐ Save $10,000 per year
- ☐ Start side business to generate income
  Put this income in savings

Short Term Steps

- ☐ Find high interest -bearing account
- ☐ Open savings account
- ☐ Create a weekly budget
- ☐ Save 30% of income for 1 year
- ☐ Don't eat out for 1 month, put savings in account

My Reward: I will reward myself at the end of each month with being able to make a small purchase (less then $100_) of something I want.

As you can see, some of the steps you take can lead you into other goals. Most times you will notice your goals will spark and become the seeds for others. This is a great thing and often a good indicator that things are in alignment. Yours may not look exactly like this, but it is a step in starting to create the goals and track them.

Here is a blank goal chart for you to create one of your goals. Pick any category and write out your goal sentence. Remember to list the goal, when it will be completed by, and write the sentence in present tense.

Goal

____

____

- ☐ **Lifetime Goal**
- ☐ **Long Term Goal**
- ☐ **Short Term Goal**

What steps do I need to take to achieve:

____

Long Term Steps

- ☐
- ☐
- ☐
- ☐
- ☐

Long Term Steps

- ☐
- ☐
- ☐
- ☐
- ☐

My Reward:

____

____

____

Now that we have set some goals, we need to take just a moment to think about what distractions or "goalkeepers" could get in the way. If we are able to identify these things upfront, we can be prepared to move right past them and accomplish our goals. I do not usually like to give energy to anything that can take me off my path, but if you are not aware of those things they can be derailing. In our same driving example of mile markers, finish lines, and watching our odometer, these "goalkeepers" can be things like flat tires, speed traps, traffic and road detours. Some of these things happen on road trips. You can have your route planned and something unexpected comes up. Being prepared is the key. Having a spare available is helpful. While you may get a flat tire, and it can be a temporary pause, getting the tire changed quickly can get you back on the road.

What are some goalkeepers in your life? Identify those things that can take you off course and prepare for them. Making this shift may seem easy at first. You're all inspired and ready to take action… and then life happens. Learn to adjust to setbacks and detours, not allowing them to completely take you off the road to your finish line. You have set the goal and you will reach it. Having a strong **WHY** will help you in reaching each finish line; it will keep fueling you along the journey. Remember motivation wears off, but that's why having multiple goals you are striving for simultaneously is important.

You may be thinking, "Candace, I'm already impressed with myself." If that is your thought, that's amazing, and I'm excited for you. However, how can we push you further? There has to be something in life, either currently or in the future, that you want to achieve or have. How do we take your current thinking and press it to the next level? One consistent question you should always have is, "what's next?" Take the time to celebrate where you are, just don't get comfortable there. Every goal you reach, every step you take should be celebrated.

There is no feat too big or too small, if you have set out to accomplish it. I used to be a supervisor at a large shipping and logistics company. Attendance was a companywide issue, especially because we worked third shift. When my team would come in on time every shift for a week, I would celebrate that with them. I made it a pretty big deal, mostly because who is celebrating the everyday things with us? We don't always know what someone had to endure to make it to work each shift, so the fact that they are here was a big deal to them and me.

Now on the other hand I am not a huge fan of rewarding myself for "simple" everyday activities unless there is a reason. If that is a struggle for you; celebrate it when you complete it. For example, making my bed. Now you may be thinking; Candace, making your bed, really?! Yes, making my bed. I *loathed* making my bed. Why, I'm just going to get right back in it later that night anyway. Then I started to realize, making my bed was accomplishing something at the start of my day. In doing so, it set the momentum for accomplishments throughout the rest of my day as well. I set a goal to make my bed every day for a month. I kept a checklist in my calendar. At the end of that month, my reward to myself was purchasing a new comforter set. I could have easily gone out and bought the set without attaching the goal, but it meant so much more when I finished the goal first. I didn't just buy it, I *earned* it. You can use these tools to start elevating your goals from small short ones, to bigger lengthier ones.

As you begin to accomplish things and start reaching your goals faster, more and more things will seem to get in the way. There will be more obstacles to overcome. Have you ever played any video games? Super Mario Brothers to be more specific. As you get closer to the end of the game, the final level, things get harder not easier. There are more things trying to stop you from making it through the final castle. But just as there are more things trying to stop you, you have picked up more tools along the way to help you.

I was born in the early 80s, which means I grew up in the 90s. During a time where video games and Hot Pockets ruled the world. Not like today's games where it's all first-person role playing; but when you had to get through a level by dodging obstacles and pitfalls to finally get to the 'boss'. Each level incorporated things you've encountered before but threw some new 'baddies' at you and you were forced to readjust, seemingly with three lives to start. This was an era before the memory cartridges and hard drive space to save your progress. Every time you turned on the console you were forced to start from the beginning.

This makes me think about life and how we are forced to start over every day. We plug in and turn on when the alarm goes off and are faced with obstacles and pitfalls all day long. We're smarter each time. We remember lessons and learn new strategies to get us through the day, but then we pass the levels we have already beaten and are faced with that 'boss'.

In the game world, you hit it three times; it dies, and you progress to the next level. It does *not* always go this smoothly. I can remember countless days of trying to beat Bowser; losing lives, shrinking, running out of power ups *just* when I need 'em the most. I would be brought almost to tears of frustration, angst and confusion (I clearly had a problem losing). But in every game every level is designed to beat it, you just have to use the right moves and combinations.

In our daily lives, these 'bosses' show up as relationships, family, dream stealers, jobs, finances and situations out of our control. We walk through the day figuring out new ways to beat it. Jump over this hurdle, pass this test, get this promotion, spend more time with our loved ones. It can become overwhelming. Being pulled in a multitude of directions, thinking you remembered what was ahead, but forgetting that one pitfall was there. Strive to get to the checkpoints. Don't be afraid to take a break and come back to it later. Luckily this is life and not a video game so you *can* save your progress. The thing to remember is, there is always a way to beat each level. You may have to lose a few lives, you may run out of power ups, or have to start this level over; but stay consistent. You can only lose the game if you quit.

The console won't work if there is no power; so, stay plugged into a Higher Power, learn from your past mistakes and you will win in this game!

As you take this journey; it's not that it gets easier, you get better. You are able to pull from circumstances that stopped you before. You now remember to jump over holes you didn't see on your first go-round. Having multiple goals, you are working towards at the same time allows you to learn skills and lessons that can help you. Whenever you feel stuck, do something new or different. You will have people in your life tell you to "slow down" or "you're doing too much." I want you to take a hard look at the source of those comments. Do they have what you are reaching for? Have they already passed the level you are reaching for? If not, take the information, let it pass by and keep going!

Overall, in life maybe we don't ever have an actual finish line. Perhaps that ultimate finish line is our last breath. You want to make sure you have passed every mile marker and done all the sightseeing you can on this journey. You are in the driver's seat, and your vehicle (life) will only go where you take it.

Let me tell you about one of the toughest but most rewarding journeys I started, I'm still on it and it's a wild ride.

It's Story Time!!

In November 2017, I started Canvases With Candace LLC. I had no idea what it could turn out to be and didn't have a plan either. I was just taking orders as they came and had one party booked for early December. There was no goal in place. I remember repeating "I'm just gonna see where this goes," over and over again. While I had built the network marketing business, I knew very little about running a small business. At this point it was just a way for me to make a few extra dollars here and there.

I did the first party and that was a success. We had 12 guests, celebrated, painted and I even had a friend come in to do some photography for me. I mean if I was going to do it, I might as well go all out. The party came to a close and I was able to ride the wave for another week or two. Energy was high, my Facebook page was gaining some traction, but no new parties yet.

At that point I decided it was time to take it more seriously and set my first few goals. I was having a New Year's Day party. I sent out tons of invites rented a venue and came up with the art and theme for the event. I planned for 30 guests and I had it set in my mind I would sell out this event. All a week or so before the actual event date. Talk about a lofty goal. I didn't do much planning and marketing the way I should have, but I didn't know any better. The day of the event arrived. I was ready, excited, and needless to say disappointed. That day I took my first big loss in business. While I stood instructing a class of seven, all of which were my friends and family, I knew I wanted this to be bigger and I was going to have to set some real goals.

After leaving that event and being in the negative, where I already didn't have the extra money to begin with, I decided not to let it break me down. I set a short-term goal to strictly promote for private events. I started creating more marketing and set a goal to have three to four parties a month. January ended and there were no more parties on the books. In February, I got a hit. Someone wanted an event and we set that one up. This was a party for eight. In my mind this was the momentum I needed. We had another party set for March, and another for April, I was on a roll; in my mind. Financially every dollar I made was going back into the business and the parties just weren't coming fast enough. By May the parties slowed down, while I still had the goal of three to four times a month, I had only done three to four for the *year*.

This is when doubt started to find its way into my mind. I started questioning if this was what I was supposed to be doing. In the midst of growing this business I finally was able to get a job that provided more stability financially. I started working in the IT field as a systems trainer. There was so much to learn at work, and my mind often wandered to how I could keep my business afloat. I went through a few weeks of changing the business model, to adjusting prices and all the while still not considering myself an artist. In my mind I wasn't an artist, I was just an art instructor.

June, July, and August rolled around and not one party was booked. I was starting to panic. I had spoken so highly, and with so much conviction, that this would be a successful business. I was starting to feel the squeeze of failure around my neck again. I searched for ways to generate some business and an opportunity for a vending event came to me. The cost was higher than I anticipated, but it was the only thing I could do to get out and introduce more people to what Canvases With Candace had to offer. I decided a few days before the event that I would sell art while talking to the customers about our parties. The only problem is three days before the event, I had no art created to sell.

The mind is a powerful thing if you allow it to be. I went to my local craft store and purchased more canvases in various sizes and got to work. I was looking for inspiration any and everywhere I could find it. In 36 hours, I painted 42 pieces ranging from 5x7 to 12x16 and was ready to set up. I had overcome the last detour only to be hit with another one. I had no idea how to set up and successfully run a vending booth. I grabbed some tablecloths, my newly created art, and showed up the day of the event.

My heart beating out of my chest each and every moment, because if my calculations were correct and I sold out of every painting I had with me, I was going to make over $2500 that day. I could hear a phrase replaying in my head all morning, "fake it 'til you make it." I was going to transform to the best art dealer they had ever seen. I brought my photographer with me and we got to work. I met people, I shook hands, I sold art, I even live painted and raffled it off. As the day came to a close and it was time to tally up all that had been made, I felt my heart sink again. I had grossly missed my mark of $2500 and was only shy by about $2350. I could have been disappointed. I could have decided that day that art sales was not my thing. What I learned that day was I could set a goal (of marathon painting) and complete it. I had now transformed from an art instructor to an artist. I took that time to readjust my goals and planned on finding more and any event where I could set up.

I took this lull in business to mean I needed to learn something. I needed to stretch myself and expand my reach. I took on a few more vending events, with fairly similar results. By this point, I was no longer disappointed in the results, but my goal had changed. It changed from the money goal to the impact goal. From the time I started the business the goal was always money. When I shifted my mindset from money to impact, I started to see more growth, not just in my business, but in myself as well. I wasn't as stressed out about the business and I decided this was a great time to reward myself and celebrate the one-year anniversary.

In September I started planning the biggest paint party I could imagine. The initial plans called for 60 guests, at an outdoor venue, with live music, poetry, and of course me instructing. I got an event planner; we created a blueprint for the event. There would be screens and platforms so all the guests could see me, there would be an abundance of food and drinks as we all celebrated the 12 months of Canvases With Candace. It was set for November 2018, a ONE-Derland Extravaganza! If you haven't noticed planning and thinking big has never been my problem. Execution and follow through, definitely an area of opportunity. My mental event and wallet did *not* agree on a lot of the details, so we had to scale it back. Again, I set a goal, and had to readjust. Another detour.

The party still went on, there were a few hiccups along the way. We had to downsize venues, downsize guest allowance and scale back on the menu, screens and platforms. But everything else came together even more magical than I could have dreamed. I stood in front of 33 guests that afternoon. Staring into their faces as I thanked them for attending and supporting me over the last year and giving them the vision of where the company is headed over the next few years. That day in front of those guests I declared growth, and more impact from my business. I never talked about how much money I wanted to make, or what didn't happen over the last year that I was anticipating. I talked about the people I have met, the stories of the hosts of the parties I instructed, and how each one touched my life in some way.

That first year in business I *planned* for financial growth but got so much more. Because of the detours and rest areas I was forced to make stops at during the first leg of the journey, I have been able to more accurately map out my second year. I could have thrown my hands up in January after leaving the New Year's Day in the hole. I could have allowed the "summer slump" of no parties or prospects to take me off the road completely. I could have allowed the drastic difference in planned sales from the August vending event, make me put my brushes and canvases away for good. I could have, but I didn't. Instead I took that year to practice my techniques in painting and instructing. I took that time to really figure out **WHY** I was in business to begin with. I took that time to find *my* inner artist and let her out.

As an artist and instructor, one of the things I teach toward the end of each event is to know when to step back and admire what you've done. Don't get caught up wanting to make it "perfect." Your brush has guided you to where you are. Allow yourself to be impressed with what you've created. You *are* the artist and your *life* is your masterpiece.

I haven't stopped making ambitious goals into this second and third year. I am pleased to say with all the lessons learned from year one, our company has been able to impact more than double the lives/people in six months compared to the first 12. I don't run into the same pitfalls and hurdles as the first year, because I was able to learn from them and see them before they happen.

#SpeakWhatYouSeek

"The best way to predict the future is to invent it."

-Alan Kay

Your voice is distinctly yours. Your voice can express more than what you *say*. The tone you use can depict your mood. The rate in which you speak can reflect your emotions. Think about it. When you're excited, usually your rate of speech gets faster and the tone of your voice gets higher. When you're sad, you speak slower and in a lower tone. If angry, it's usually louder and often times deeper. When you're confused, it can be more deliberate and choppier. Just by your voice someone can usually tell what mood you're in even if your body language doesn't match. Have you ever sent someone a text, or an email and they told you they can hear your voice while reading your words? Our voices are essentially our audible fingerprint.

When you speak, you set a chain reaction with the Universe. The Universe is a series of vibrations, and your voice can either resonate with those vibrations, or disrupt them. Because of this connection with the Universe and its frequencies we are able to use that voice to speak into existence that which we desire or bring on more of what we deflect. Your voice is in essence a reflection of your inner being; your soul.

Have you heard the expression, "It's not what you say, but how you say it?" I want you to try an exercise really quick.

Envision you are seeing your very best female friend in the whole world, whom you haven't seen in months. Or your favorite female celebrity whom, you've always wanted to meet. You can feel the excitement brewing inside, a huge smile comes across your face. All 32 teeth are pretty much showing, and you say "Hey, how are you?" Go ahead, say it out loud. How did it come out? Was your tone higher than you normally speak? Did you drag your "hey" out just a little bit longer? Could you feel your smile as you spoke?

Now imagine you are seeing the person you dislike the *most* on this planet. Someone who just gets under your skin. Think about an ex, or a former mean boss. You are seeing them for the first time in months, and they seem excited to see you and approach you with a huge smile and say hi. Respond out loud with "Hey, how are you?" How did you sound this time? Was your tone flatter? Did you slump your shoulders down a bit, and drop your voice too? Was it more of an annoyed whisper? Almost like you were speaking through gritted teeth. Yeah, I'm sure it was.

Neither of those scenarios are taking place right now, however, you were able to let your mind envision both. Your body physically changed within an instant, to say the exact same thing in two completely different ways. You said them differently because there was emotion attached and that emotion set off a vibrational shift to your voice. There was an actual exchange of energy even though you were the only person in the room. When your mind and your voice combine their powers, no you don't turn into Captain Planet, but you are able to physically and metaphysically alter your current state.

Now we are going to flip it. I want you to say "Hey, how are you" to your best friend as if they were your that person you dislike. Even though you can see your best friend in your mind, I want you to concentrate as if they were the person you disliked. Your words didn't come out the same as the first time, did they. Granted they probably weren't as tight lipped as the first example with your nemesis, but they definitely weren't as jovial as your first one either. Now say "Hey, how are you" to the person you dislike as if they were your best friend. Use your mind to see you saying it in a good mood and tone. Did it work? Again, probably not as exciting as the first time, but surely not as vexed as the first time either. You were able to use your *mind* to alter your physical state and that transformed through your voice. Do you realize how *powerful* you are?

Something I heard a few years ago, has become my mantra on a daily basis. "Speak what you seek, until you see what you've said." When you start to change your narrative, you start to change your life. When you are learning something and say "Oh, I know that." You have instantly cut your brain off from absorbing any new information. You have flipped the switch with the Universe and turned off your vibrations. When you use words like can't and try, you are negating possibilities.

For example, take Baby Boomers. They didn't grow up like millennials with full access to technology, and instant gratification. Most will tell you that technology is "too hard" and they are "too old to learn anything new." Those two statements alone disconnect them from the ability to enhance their current skills. We all know at least one Baby Boomer, who has been able to move with the ebbs and flows of current tech advances. Learning anything new can be difficult, but not impossible.

Imagine them taking that same language and reversing it, "Technology is new but I am ready to learn and master it." By changing that narrative, they are now open to the new information and willing to keep working towards the goal of learning and inevitably mastering the skill. They have created an affirmation for themselves specifically by using two of the smallest words in the English Dictionary, "I Am."

Anytime you start a sentence with the words "I Am..." you are affirming the words that follow to be true. They are typically said in the present tense. As we saw in our exercise, you can physically change your current circumstances and emotional energy with words and thoughts. Have you ever seen a toddler fall, and not cry immediately; the parent typically does one of two things. They either run over and say "Oh no are you ok?" It's in a concerned, hurried, and slightly panicked tone. From there the toddler who wasn't crying yet, is now wailing and answers back through tears, "noooooo." The other response is usually, "You're ok." This is said in an affirming, positive, reinforcing way. Letting the toddler know they *are* okay and not hurt. Startled, sure, but not hurt. This toddler will usually get up repeat the words "I'm ok" and continue on with their activity. Just the tone of the trusted adult had the power to alter the physical and emotional state of the child, and their response further substantiated their feelings.

Your brain will do exactly what you tell it to do. If you are afraid, repeating "I am not afraid" has the power to calm your heart rate, slow your breathing and give you more confidence as you start to believe what you are saying. You are speaking your bravery until you indeed see and feel your bravery. Have you ever seen someone who is drunk; they may not realize they are going to probably have a massive hangover the next morning. In that moment they are repeating, "I am having so much fun" over and over again. So much that they *are* having fun even if the people around them aren't. Come on, we have all been that person at least once in our lives, right?!

These components we are speaking about are all elements of a popular documentary and a book titled *The Secret*. You can find it on most streaming sites, or book seller outlets, if you haven't watched/read it before. I sat for the first time and watched the documentary and was floored at how much of my life I had willed into existence; both good and bad. Now of course there are some things that are out of our control, however the one thing we have explicit control over is ourselves. While I usually thought of myself as a positive person. Someone who is fairly optimistic and sees the glass as half full; I realized I was fighting against myself, with my thoughts and words. For this exercise, I encourage you to carve out time to read or watch *The Secret*. Then begin implementing its teachings into your life as well.

What it speaks about is the power of your thoughts, and how what you think about expands. Also due to the vibrations we've been talking about. One of the examples that resonated with me the most was cars. Have you ever wanted or had a "dream car?" You think about that car so much, you see it everywhere. The same color, make, model, style. It's almost as if everyone went out and got that specific car to taunt you. On the other hand, have you ever purchased a car you didn't expect to buy, and all of a sudden while you never saw them before you see them all the time now? That again is the power of your thoughts. You own the car, see it, drive it daily; now you are focused on it, even subconsciously. Now you see it everywhere.

Remember when I told you I earned the luxury car? Prior to owning it, it was the only car I ever really wanted from my teenage years. I saw it everywhere for years. When I got it, I would see the same make and model in almost every parking lot I went to. I was starting to think there was some sale, buy one get one free going on. They were everywhere. When I lost it, I stopped thinking about it. And now that I think about it now, I hardly *ever* see that car on the road anymore. I still go to the same places I did before. I still park in the same lots, but my mind isn't tuned into that image as it used to be. There may still be tons of them on the road every day, but I don't notice them anymore. My subconscious let the tie go.

Around the time I was introduced to *The Secret* I also started listening to hours and hours of personal development audios. Learning that what you download into your brain is going to be what is produced as well. I took an active stand at putting good information in; podcasts, YouTube videos, audiobooks. If it was about "self-help" and being a better person, I was all over it. You'll start to see it's very real. What you listen to, what you watch, they all play a major role in how you approach your everyday. It will put a spotlight on yourself and those around you. You will really be able to identify three types of attitudes: pessimistic, optimistic, and those who consider themselves realists.

Pessimistic people are the ones who have a problem for every solution. It doesn't matter the odds, they will always, and I mean always, take the lesser option. They typically don't take responsibility for anything happening to them, or what their part in a situation is. As we've just learned, what you focus on expands. If you are constantly thinking something bad is going to happen, guess what? Hello, you've basically invited misfortune right to your front door. To an optimistic person and a realist, the pessimist is the hardest to be around, or they can spark questions of uncertainty and doubt in the realist. Let's not get too far ahead.

The optimist is the person who is the troubleshooter. They are the problem solver, and usually won't necessarily rely on logic, but sheer willpower to move through scenarios. They will find the silver lining even when all signs point to something else. Somehow, through it all they are able to see either the lesson, or the light even in dark situations. They can often be seen as aloof or "dreamers" especially by pessimists and realists.

In my opinion, the realist is the toughest of the three, because they are the beautiful yet tragic blend of both the optimist and pessimist. They will often explain their logic with "I'm just prepared for anything." They usually wane on the side of optimism, but will also give you every reason why things could go wrong, and then follow it up with "I do really want -insert what they want- but I just know things happen so I don't want to set myself up for disappointment." Language like this is really confusing to the Universe.

I don't believe there is a right or wrong way to be when considering these three types of people. I do however believe that whichever you are, you don't have to stay that way if you don't want to. You can begin to transform and manifest whatever you desire by changing the way you look at things. Your attitude is completely up to you. You can wake up in an instant and decide you are going to stop focusing on what could go wrong and start positioning your thoughts towards what you want.

I can remember once applying for a job, a friend told me about. I really wanted this job. It was a vast pay increase; it was in alignment with what I wanted to do professionally. She told me about the position and explained that she didn't want it and thought I'd be a good fit. I applied for it; didn't hear anything back. I waited and waited, nothing. Then a few weeks later my friend came to me telling me she got a new job and it was *that* one. In the initial moment I wanted to be upset, like "why would you tell me about the job if you were applying too." I immediately stopped my thoughts and redirected to being happy for her. She was qualified for the position and didn't have to share the information with me to begin with. I instantly transformed my thoughts and energy to repeating, "what is for you is for you and you will be ready when the job for you is available." I repeated that a few times in my head and stopped thinking about it. I refocused my energy on gaining more skills in my field. A few short weeks later, I got a phone call from the same company offering me a position that was even *more* aligned with my career goals, and this time I was ready! I believe that job became available to me in *my* time because I allowed my thoughts to send a positive vibration back to the universe. I could have been upset and salty about it, but I didn't.

This happens to us every day. Someone cut us off while driving. Pulled into a parking spot we were waiting for. Left out information that could have been imperative to us, but perhaps not to them. Stood us up for a meeting; I mean the list of things that happen on a daily basis can go on. You get the point. We don't have to allow everything to pull us into their orbit. Keep your energy and universe centered on you.

Affirmations. So now that we know how they work, do you already use them? I remember watching the tv show Being Mary Jane with Gabrielle Union, and the main character had sticky notes posted all around her bedroom with quotes and affirmations. When I took a deep dive into understanding manifestation, I took my goals, my affirmations, and dreams and put them on 3x5 index cards and started placing them all around my house. I created an environment where I saw positivity every day. Even now at my job I keep small notes and reminders of positivity posted around my cubicle. What are a few positive thoughts or affirmations you have in your space? Have you created an environment where you can see and repeat that which you desire on a daily basis? If you do, awesome we're going to make some more. If you don't, that's great too, because we will get you started.

I create my affirmations specifically for things that I am working through. I make a point not to use the negative tense of the word, but whatever the positive opposite is. Let me give you an example. Getting out of bed in the mornings can be difficult, especially if you've stayed up late the night before, as I often do as a creator. I could say, "I am a person who doesn't have a hard time getting out of bed." Instead I say exactly what I want to feel or behave as when I wake up, "I wake up and greet the day with excitement and energy." Making that switch now programs my brain to decide how I will wake up and what my mood will be. It counteracts what may be physically feeling because my brain is my control center and tells my body what to do.

An affirmation like this, well any affirmation for that matter, will take more than once to activate. I make this a part of my daily routine so that it becomes habit. Saying these affirmations don't stop things from happening through the day to take us off track, but they allow you to refocus and stay in control. With my art at one point didn't *feel* like an artist, I had to manifest it by repeating, "I am an artist I create masterpieces."

What are some things you may struggle with that you need to affirm the opposite and positive energy? List a few ideas below.

a. Currently I want to change

____

b. Currently I want to change

____

c. Currently I want to change

____

d. Currently I want to change

____

e. Currently I want to change

____

Now let's turn those into affirmations.
Set yours up like this:
Currently I want to change <u>my eating habits</u> ... I eat food that fuels and heals my body.
Currently I want to change <u>my career</u>... I have a career that fulfills me and aligns with my goals.
Currently I want to change <u>my financial status</u>... I am financially prepared and fiscally sound.

Your turn. Remember to start each sentence with "I" or "I am". Use words that describe what and/or how you have already achieved your result in the present tense.

a. ____

b. ____

c. ____

d. ____

e. ____

For the next 24 hours. I want you to repeat these five affirmations. Start with saying each of them as soon as you wake up. Say them again when you are on your morning commute. Again, in the middle of your day. On your evening commute. Then lastly right before you go to bed. When you say them you must say them aloud? If you can look at yourself in the mirror when you say them do that as well. Please, not while you are driving, unless you're at a red light. Say them as if they are currently happening. Most importantly say them with confidence and believe in yourself when you say them. I can almost guarantee, you will wake up after that 24 hours feeling different. Once you have committed these affirmations into your daily routine, start making other ones. If you're feeling especially ambitious, start making little notes to yourself in various places. I used to keep my health and weight affirmations attached to the fridge. Every time I went in I had to read that affirmation first, "I eat food that fuels and heals my body."

Here are a few categories or prompts for your affirmations:

Affirmation Categories				
Abundance	Appreciation	Attitude	Balance	Beauty
Career	Confidence	Compassion	Determination	Dreams
Emotions	Energy	Exercise	Faith	Family
Favor	Fear	Friendship	Grace	Gratitude
Happiness	Healing	Hope	Inner self	Joy
Love	Marriage	Money	Passion	Peace
Power	Pride	Purpose	Relationships	Respect
Self-Esteem	Self-Image	Spiritual	Strength	Success
Thoughts	Trust	Wealth	Weight	Work

Creating affirmations allows you to begin to solidify your vision for yourself. Maybe you are the person who has had everyone around you dictate what to do, and how to do it. Maybe you are the person who has not really thought about your life over the next five to ten years. You could be a person who thinks about these things often but aren't producing. You could even be the person who has so many ideas you don't even know where to begin. Something that helped me was vision boards.

Vision boards are another great way to keep your focus on what you want. There are tons of ideas and recommendations on how to create vision boards. Some people see them as simply "craft time" by cutting out pictures from magazines of things you want. That is a great way to start. If you don't know what you want, how can you instruct the universe to make it available to you? Using vision boards is a great way to jumpstart that thought process and spark ideas. In December each year, I sit down and review what I have from my vision board that year and see what I have accomplished and what it still left. I will usually take what is left and add to the new year vision board. Also, that is a great time for me to reflect on what I have learned or what may have changed for me in what I still desire.

I have taken pictures of vision boards that I've created and kept them in places where I can see them often. The website Pinterest is a great place to digitally store images and ideas such as this.

With vision boards you are essentially doing the same activity as creating affirmations, just usually in image form. You can create the board for one area of life, or a multitude. I know some people who only make them for their career goals, or travel goals. Some make them for their health and wellness goals. The beauty of a vision board is it's *your* vision so there is truly no right or wrong way to do it. You just have to do it. You can use magazines and find words you like and resonate with. You can print off images you've searched for on the internet. You can use actual pictures of yourself, or just use a marker and write what you want. You will start to notice as you go on through your year, how many things you start to check off simply because you can see it in front of you. My biggest suggestion is to make sure you are using positive words, empowering photos, and place it somewhere you can see it often.

It's Story Time!!

I have always been a reader. I was the kid who stayed up late with a flashlight under my covers reading Encyclopedia Brown. Summers were filled with reading challenges, frequent trips to the library, and learning new words. As I got older those books changed to books by Eric Jerome Dickey, Omar Tyree and even Zane. I would get so lost in the stories, building connections to these characters and wondering what my life would be like in my 20s like they were. Fast forward to college, I mainly only read for class, but still had a love for words. Their meanings, their effect, their sound.

After graduating college and starting in my career I was introduced to the world of personal development. This was a different type of reading. I felt my soul get full when I would read these books. The first book I was introduced to was <u>Rich Dad Poor Dad</u> (RDPD) by Robert Kiyosaki. I read this book in about two hours. I couldn't put it down. I was opening my mind in ways I wasn't fully exposed to, or when I was exposed, I wasn't ready to learn. I started looking at how I approached my life, my work and my finances in a completely different way. My idea of "successful" for so long was to make a mid-five-figure salary, have a decent car and house and basically afford regular life. These books started opening my mind to so much more.

The next book I read was <u>Secrets of the Millionaire Mind</u> (SMM) By T. Harv Eker. I thought I learned something with

RDPD; SMM blew my mind wide open. These principles he teaches in the book showed me I deserved so much more than a mid-five-figure salary. It taught me there was more to wealth than just money. From reading those two books alone, I made a decision entrepreneurship was my desire and I would stop at nothing until I achieved my level of success and overall wealth.

Someone I have always considered a "virtual mentor," like most young black girls, is Oprah. I heard an interview with Oprah saying she had read <u>Think and Grow Rich</u> (TGR) by Napoleon Hill over 15 times. Can you guess what my next bookstore haul had included? You guessed it, TGR. I opened the book, read three pages and put it down. The language was so antiquated. It was like reading really bad Shakespeare. I started picking up books weekly at the bookstore. At this time, I was commuting by train every day for about an hour, so I could read a book a week if not more.

I was satisfying my craving for words like I had always done, but these words had some flavor! I began making vision boards, filling my home with positivity, and eliminated anything that wasn't aligned with my personal growth. I even stopped watching TV. That as hard, mostly because my partner at the time was a reality junky. I would start to detach during TV time and kept working on myself.

Then I was introduced to the world of audio. Not audiobooks, but recorded presentations and speeches by people like Les Brown, Jim Rohn and Eric Thomas. The audio that changed my life completely was *The Strangest Secret* by Earl Nightingale. Now he actually sounds like

TGR read, but once you get past the old school radio voice; the message is powerful. He references TGR in the 30 min recording, which prompted me to go back and pick it up again. I picked it up after a few months of it sitting on the shelf and finished it in about a week. To date I have read it three times now. Only 13 more times to pass Oprah.

These books and audios started exercising my mind. Over time, about six or seven years, I had consumed so much information I could almost regurgitate just about any specific line from either a book or an audio recording. How did this help me? Well, it always gave me confidence to speak to anyone in any setting. Whether I was knowledgeable in the subject or not, I never felt I didn't belong in the room. It started transforming me from the inside out and it was outwardly noticeable. I would hear comments like, "Wow, Candace you just look different; happier" I can remember once being told, "When I first met you I thought there had to be something fake about you, there is no way you were just that happy of a person. Then as I got to know you more, I realized, yeah you really are."

While there were many days that were tough through my journey, I am a believer that doing so much personal development when I did, allowed me to fall, but not stay down. It gave me almost a protective coating around my mind and heart. While I was hurting, while I was struggling, and at times felt so lost; I knew ultimately it wouldn't last forever. I had to go back to my teachings and relearn a few key things, but this time the learning curve was much shorter. I was able to reinvent my mentality, which honestly now makes me feel pretty incredible. I take an approach to life now where I don't know what I'm not capable of doing. Everything I am doing has been done in some form before, so why shouldn't I be able to as well? I speak with such conviction in everything I approach. I have built a belief in myself that is so deeply rooted. I know storms may come, and the wind may blow. I may bend, but I won't ever break.

I want you to be able to build that same root system within your mind. Here is my list of seeds:

<u>Books</u>	**<u>Audio Recordings</u>**
Think and Grow Rich by Napolean Hill The Compound Effect by Darren Hardy The Alchemist by Paulo Coelho The 10x Rule by Grand Cardone Start With Why by Simon Sinek How to Win Friends and Influence People by Dail Carnegie The Four Agreements by Don Miguel Ruiz Rich Dad Poor Dad by Rober Kiyosaki What to Say When You Talk to Yourself by Shad Helmstetter The Secrets of the Millionaire Mind by T. Harv Eker	Les Brown Tony Robbins John C. Maxwell Eric Thomas Jim Rohn Earl Nightingale Simon Sinek

#UpwardSpiral

"Nothing can stop me, I'm all the way up."

-Fat Joe

Welcome, you made it. This is where you get to set **YOUR** new standard. Up until this point, someone or something else has assisted you in setting the standard you have for yourself. Who or what have been your major influences? Has it been your friends and family? A spouse? Employers? Maybe society as a whole started to shape how you see yourself. All that changes today.

Recently your standards have started to change for yourself. You can physically feel the shift happening. Your mind is clearer. You have ideas and you are executing them without flaw. Doors are opening that you didn't even realize were there. You've been engaged in your personal development. Working towards your goals and using your affirmations daily. Your spiral is starting to invert. What was once facing downward is now climbing. You have a refreshed look at yourself, and others are starting to notice too. They noticed before, but this time, what they notice doesn't really affect you. You have started making this change for you.

Have you always known what your "it" factor is? Your "it" factor is the attribute that is so unique to you, no one else could replicate it. It's not even something that can be described. It's not a feeling, but more of an energy. It is your magnet pull on others. Remember, we exist in a universe of wavelengths and frequencies. Like our DNA, your wavelength has its own rhythm. If there had to be a quantifier, it would most likely be a recipe combining confidence, compassion, charm, wit and your overall aura. This will continue to grow overtime. And consistently moving up your spiral is how you can enhance that "it" factor.

Speaking of your upward spiral. What does that look like for you? When I think of it, this is what I see:

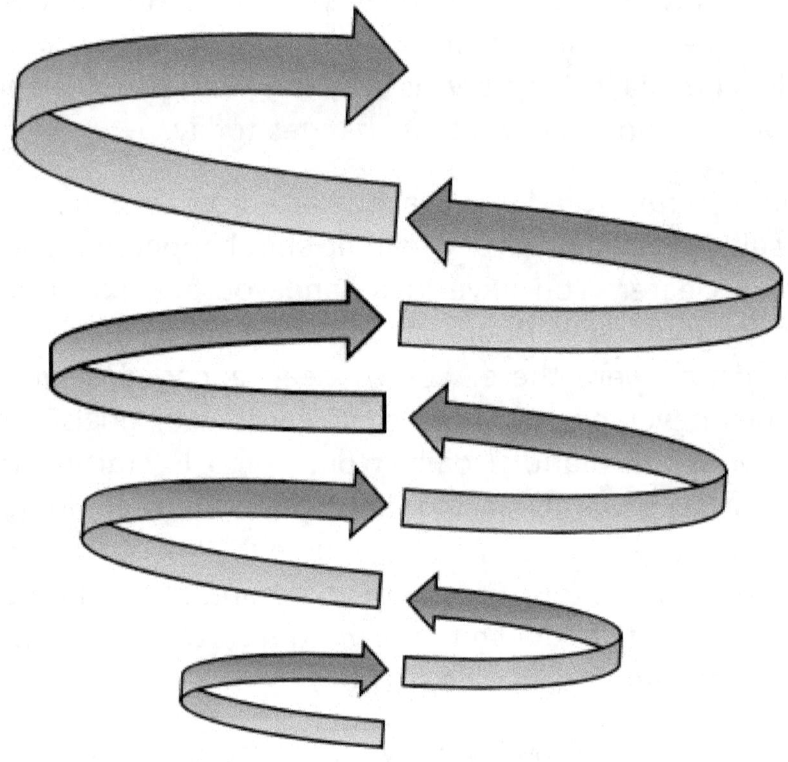

Looking at the bottom of the image, there is a distinct starting point. The spiral continues around, and the layers get bigger and longer. That means it can hold more. As you ascend up the spiral you are able to increase your efforts. You can take on more challenges and find more intricate ways to impress yourself. Every experience you are having even right now is preparing you for the next level of your spiral. While you are on level one of your spiral, you could be learning or experiencing something that will be perfectly aligned where you need it to be on level four of your spiral. Level four may be four years from now. Due to the mental clarity you now have you are able to identify when to use the lesson. I like to think of it like a chain reaction.

That makes me think about my own shift. It's **Story Time**!

I have given you every detail of that two to three-year period. I've told you all about what I learned as a result but let me tell you what was the catalyst to *my* spiral inverting.

On July 3, 2016 my relationship of six years ended. At this point I had been out of work for about six months. I was just starting to come out my fog. Seven days prior I had just hit the submit button paying for a 10-day vacation to Greece for us. The relationship had been a little rocky over the last year. Communication was as clear as mud, and we were essentially roommates at this point. I remember reading messages in their cell phone where the group conversation was spent making fun of my weight, my hair cut, my finances and my obvious depression. I will not discount I was just as responsible for our demise, but reading those words... It felt like an odd mix of being punched in the stomach, slapped in the face and having the wind knocked out of you all at once.

I have a passage from a journal entry I wrote that day which says,

"Today is the day I take control BACK! No longer will I live a life unsatisfied. I will be at my optimal health. I will get my finances 100% in order. I will regain my vision. I will pour into ME! I will maximize my personal development. I will be BETTER THAN I EVER HAVE. My ultimate goal is to be at peace with myself, eliminate toxic feelings, elements, and energies from my life. Unlearn negative and harmful practices and thought patterns, stop checking for people that don't check for me. Create a space for myself that is nurturing for growth so that I may generate loving energy for myself and others. Nourish my spirit and balance my energies. I have big dreams and I deserve to live a life I love and let that love radiate."

After writing that passage, I vividly remember crying myself to sleep for a few days. I made a declaration; I gave myself permission to hurt in the moment. I allowed myself to feel what I needed to feel, so that I could know what I never wanted to feel again. After a few days of hibernation and licking my wounds, I got up. I cleaned my house. I packed away every remnant of them and I sat down to write in that same journal. The concept of impress yourself and the upward spiral came from that entry. At the top of the page it says, "500 Things I want In Life" in big bold letters. I sat at that table that evening and started writing feverishly. Ideas were popping into my head left and right. I gave myself permission to be as "outlandish" as I could dream up. I wrote for what seemed like hours. I sat back and looked at my list. After counting them up, I had only written 38 things. How in the world was I going to come up with 500? It took me that long to make *this* list. Wanna hear what's on it?

Some of the things on the list are:

1. A 5000 sq. ft house with a balcony off my bedroom and a pool and outdoor living room
2. Write multiple books
3. Own a yacht
4. Take a private jet
5. Live abroad for 3-6 months
6. Win a speech contest
7. Have 10 streams of income
8. Regular massage visits
9. Buy a private island
10. Be a featured speaker on a popular day time television show

In writing this list, I was all over the place. But it felt great. It felt amazing to just put it on the paper. How dare I dream of having 10 streams of income when currently I didn't have one. How? The woman who lives in that list, didn't share the same current circumstances as I did. The woman in the list had already overcome what I was going through. The woman in the list was on a much higher revolution on that spiral. I was just getting started. But the beautiful thing about it was, I was starting.

Even as I sit here with you now and I look at this list, I'm already becoming that woman. I have already been able to cross things off this list. I have won a speech contest, I am on my way to building 10 streams of income, and I have written a book. That day at the table I couldn't fathom how I would ever achieve some of these things, yet here I am. Was it all a breeze from the moment I wrote my declaration? No. Did I start making my revolutions around my spiral without a speed bump or just plain roadblock? No. I scraped up my proverbial knees, quite a few times after making that list. Truthfully, until I started compiling thoughts to share with you, I had almost forgotten about the list.

Because I had so much belief in what *could be* the day, I sat down to write this list, they have already started coming true, and will continue.

Due to some of my own personal experiences, I wholeheartedly believe if there is a lesson you are supposed to learn but didn't; you will relive that same experience in various ways until you learn the lesson. If you learn the lesson the first time around; golden ticket to the next rotation. That's how spirals work. Now you have the tools to know how to control the direction of your spiral.

Use the space below to start on your Upward Spiral. This is your list of things that are impressive to you. It does not matter if they are "conceivable" at this exact moment or what is even "possible". What is the ultimate life you want for yourself? You saw the things on my list. Go big! Really reach for these. These can be emotional, physical,

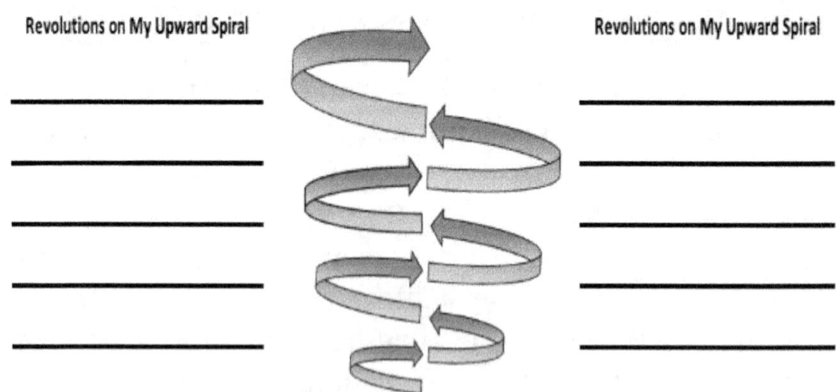

financial, actions, accolades, adventures. It is a completely blank page ready for you to write. You are the designer of *this* Upward Spiral.

#ImpressYourself

#ImpressYourself

"The journey of a thousand miles begins with one step."

-Lao Tzu

We have been taught for so long to not "brag" on ourselves. I believe we were taught that as to not put someone else down in the process. This is the difference between being confident and arrogant. I once heard it explained that arrogance means, "I'm better than you." While confidence says, "No one is better than me." Don't get the two confused. You can be confident. You will need to have those moments where you pat yourself on the back, because not always will someone do it for you.

If you are not easily impressed with other people, it may be a little more difficult for you to be impressed with yourself as well. You may be the type to hold yourself to a higher standard, and that's great. There is a distinct difference between not getting comfortable in one place while pushing yourself to your next level and not taking the time to show yourself some appreciation. Allow yourself the time to look in the mirror every now and again and say, "I am proud of you. I'm impressed with you." You must talk to yourself in this way every so often. We have so many outside things telling us we aren't "good enough," by whose standards I still will never know, but you are *more* than enough. You have something about you that makes you completely unique. You have a strength that no one else has. You have a talent that someone goes to bed at night praying for. Unleash that inner superstar, by *your* standards.

What do you think you measure yourself against on a regular basis? There are so many stimuli in our society that cause us to look to the left and the right of us and size ourselves up. Who's making the most money, who has the best relationship, who has the biggest house, who is the most attractive. We could go on for days with how society has a standard we should conform to. Did you know, you don't have to? No seriously, you don't have to. There is no rule that says your competition has to be anyone other than who stares back at you in the mirror.

We have all experienced the various types of internal experiences. Times where our facial expressions were not a true reflection of our inner feelings of self-worth. We all walk this earth just "trying to figure it out." There is no specific handbook to guide you every step of the way. However, you can choose everyday as a new opportunity to impress yourself. You will start to see your chin get a little higher; and your stance a little stronger. What does it take to impress yourself? That definition is solely up to you. What *would* impress you? You don't have to answer now. Let that marinate for now.

If we are designed to be our own competition, what would you compete against yourself in? What are you good at? And not just regular good, but exceptionally good; no, great at? What is the thing that people comment about the most? You may not even think it's something you are great at, because you've been doing it for so long. It may be something that comes natural to you so it's not even on your radar. As a training professional, I realize that as adults we typically spend more time worrying about what we don't know. Instead of harnessing the power of what we *do* know. Most of that stems simply from childhood. We were told what we did wrong or didn't know all through school. Can you think of a single teacher who would grade papers based on how many you got right, versus how many you got wrong? Even now, as we talked about "to do lists," we think of all the things we had listed that we didn't finish, but rarely do we recognize the number of things we did finish.

Have you ever found yourself dimming your light to be able to let someone else shine? This is the person who wants to know about your experiences. Then in the midst they take your experience and flip it to how something didn't work out for them. Over time when you talk to them or spend time with them you start to say less and less about things that are progressing for you. You're starting to listen to your positive audios; reading uplifting books. You share it with them because you think it will help them, like it helped you. Yet somehow, they are still able to make their candle of negativity shine brighter than your beacon of positivity. So, you say less and less about what you are doing to progress and transform your life. Or worse, you find yourself sharing horror stories of "who's life is hardest." When you have that type of energy in your circle, you have to change the circle. A mentor once told me to change your friends or *change* your friends. One of you will influence the other. Who will it be?

With elevation comes separation. As this distance starts to form, you may find yourself feeling a little bit lonely. When I first started my personal development journey, I felt the void of friendship. My books and audios became my friends, until I started surrounding myself with more people who shared the same mentality. These conversations were so different. We would have verbal battles about how many books we've read this month. How many seminars we attended, and what motivational audio was currently on repeat. We did not get caught in conversations of things that did not turn out well, unless we also shared what we learned or gained from the experience. These friends were growing with me. I needed that energy until I was strong enough to do it alone. Never in those circles did I feel compelled to subconsciously compare myself.

When you start to see yourself as your own competition, tasks that used to feel like chores now become benchmarks. I'm pretty sure this theory is why CrossFit is so popular. You do workouts to compete against your own best records, no one else's. You get to walk away with the accomplishment of knowing you were better today than any other day behind you. This concept is why I think being impressed with yourself is difficult.

We are so hard on ourselves. We reach a certain level, and if anything knocks us down a peg or two, we can get stuck. We can dwell in the idea of everything that went wrong and if we could go back what would we do differently. We allow ourselves to be consumed with the "used to be" instead of charging forward. I told you about losing my job. I thought I was on top of the world at that point. Because I wasn't thinking bigger, I didn't realize I could and would eventually surpass that level in life. I would have more, be more, do more than I even imagined at that time. Do you know anyone who spends more time talking about what they used to have or what they used to do? Are you that person? Like I said, I was.

It took a year of...well let me break it down for you. It is a little early; but it's **Story Time**!!

2017 started as a continuance of 2016. It was a year of transition, growth, unmasking, loss and light. I had some major setbacks in 2017 and they seemed to roll in every month back to back. In January, I moved out of my apartment. I released myself of my version of ultimate freedom and space, and at 32 years old moved back in with my parents. Curfew and all. In February, I quit a job because I thought they would fire me anyway. Due to where I was emotionally ending 2016, I had racked up a good amount of absences. Moving to the complete opposite side of town, with little to no motivation was not a good recipe for being on time going forward. In March I was diagnosed with jaundice, causing me to look like a walking Jack-o-lantern with no idea what caused it - as per doctors. I nearly lost my life due to the toxin levels in my liver. I became a human pin cushion for the next several weeks as my liver levels were monitored with multiple blood tests and panels, ultrasounds and screenings.

In April, my once flawless skin took a nosedive due to the hormonal changes with jaundice and rapidly growing fibroids. I acquired adult acne, something I never experienced as an adolescent. Nothing I used was working and it seemed to be getting worse day by day. In May, I was in *my* first car accident, which felt like a movie. Cue late night, rain and tow trucks. I've been in accidents before. It had always been as a passenger or at the fault of another car. Not this one. This one involved a huge rock and a pothole. Luckily, I made it out unscathed; but my Storm, that was the name of my BMW, was out of commission for a few weeks. I was now reliant on other people to get me from here to there, so let's just pile on the loss of dignity. Seems like the universe decided to let me off the hook for June. Thanks, because that was a pretty tough first half of the year.

In July, I experienced the death of someone in my family for the first time, as my Paternal Grandfather ascended onto his resting place. I was working for an insurance claims company at the time and was given the news right as I was walking out the door for work. First three calls of the morning were people calling in to claim the policy for someone who passed away. We had a special line for those calls, so they shouldn't have been routed to my phone, however here we were. I tried to take the calls while crying uncontrollably and was sent home.

On top of that, I had to miss the funeral due to a doctor's appointment that could not be rescheduled. It was a pre-surgery appointment. A few days later in August, I had my first major surgery. A laparoscopic myomectomy, to have a four-and-a-half-pound fibroid removed. With living most of my twenties being told I'd probably never be able to conceive children; I went to a reproductive endocrinologist to inquire about cryopreservation of my eggs. I was able to find a specialist to perform the surgery, I was told for years was impossible. Recovery was the longest four weeks ever and painful. Yet this was my first glimpse of a break in the clouds.

In September, I changed careers back to sales. This time it was 100% commission, and I thought it would be a great transition. Over the years I had done the personal development needed to have the right mental stability for sales. There were people who believed in me and wanted to see me grow. They were impressed with me before I had even made my first sale. I spoke so much about what I *used* to do and how good I *used* to be. I was still stuck and trying to recreate the life I *used* to have. I flopped, hard. I quickly found myself, again, struggling financially. I could see the disappointment in my parents' eyes and hear it in their voices. They believed me when I said this time would be different. Nevertheless, here we were. In October, I found myself consumed with taking on emotional struggles, after learning of a tragedy happening to someone close to me. I can remember sitting in a cationic state for nearly three days. Literally stuck and so emotionally heavy. With all I was already dealing with I was foolishly taking on someone else's baggage.

In November, I lost my car due to financial mismanagement and had been stripped down to the very simplest form of adulthood. I was living at home, parents now so disappointed in what I allowed to happen. I was working very part-time and barely bringing in enough money to do anything for myself. I was now completely dependent on everyone around me, when I was so used to being the strong one. Every bit of personal development I had ever done seemed to fly out the window. I was ready to turn my back on the world, because I felt the world turned its back on me.

You could break these events up over the course of ten years. Individually these things are enough to send anyone into a downward spiral of destruction, however somehow, I was able to push through. I look back on these instances of tumultuous encounters, and situations and know that I survived. It would be really easy to say this was hands down the worst year of my life, but I don't want to take away from the lessons I've learned in hindsight.

In January, I learned how to ask for help, where I was afraid to before. By going to my parents and asking them to let me move back home, I learned humility and that family will always be there for you. In February, I learned to not react due to what I *think* may happen. I learned to be more proactive in my decision making and stay in control of my actions. In March, I learned how important my health is and to not take any moment for granted. I learned to listen to my body, and I am now more in tune.

In April, I learned that beauty is only skin deep. What you look like physically does not have a true bearing on who you are inside. I learned I won't always be able to rely on a "pretty face" to get me through situations. In May, I learned that material things can be lost and replaced, and life can be spared instead of sacrificed. I also learned to be more aware of what's around me. In June, I learned that even every storm has a break, and it won't always be bad forever.

In July, I was reminded to always "Be Sweet," as Grandpa Wilbur would say. I learned to take the time to spend quality time with those around you. Cherish the moments you have together and create as many memories as you can. You never know when their last day, or yours, will come. In August, I learned in some instances second and sometimes third opinions matter. Keep searching for information and alternatives until you find what can help you. In September, I learned that not everything goes as planned, but every experience you have will prepare you for the future *if* you pay attention. I currently am working back for the sales company, but in a different capacity, and it was in part some of my experience then that prepared me for the position now.

In October I learned that everyone wears a mask, and only light can cast away darkness. Keep those you love, close to you and rely on your intuition. There is no such thing as a good secret. Ultimately, in November, I learned the most organic lesson in responsibility. There will not always be a safety net in life. While you should take chances, remember to be smart and secure what you can. One day someone told me, "Candace, you know cars get repossessed all the time." Now that didn't give me a pass for myself, but it gave me the permission I needed to stop beating myself up about it. From that moment forward I was no longer bound to the idea of what happened to me. I made a decision that I wouldn't put myself in position to have it happen again.

2017 wasn't a year to brag about, but it was necessary to create the experiences I needed to be able to learn and grow from. I took a lot of these lessons, while not that long ago, and currently apply them to my life.

Through those experiences I had plenty of people with opinions, said and not said. I was given advice when I didn't ask for it, instruction when I didn't seek it and pity when I didn't want it. I was juggling so many things, trying to keep so many people happy and impressed. In the process, I forgot about the most important part of the whole equation; me. I had allowed my standards for myself to fall so low because I stopped caring at some point. I was just moving through each day with no goal, no plan, no focus. Just existing.

Have you ever felt like that? Like you were just existing, or even on a downward spiral? If you have, it is okay. You've either come out of that fog, or you *are* coming out of it. Releasing the bondage of your past can feel like one of the hardest things to do, but only if you have no vision of where you can and *will* be. So, what does it really take to impress yourself. How do you even begin? Here are the **Five Steps to Impress Yourself.**

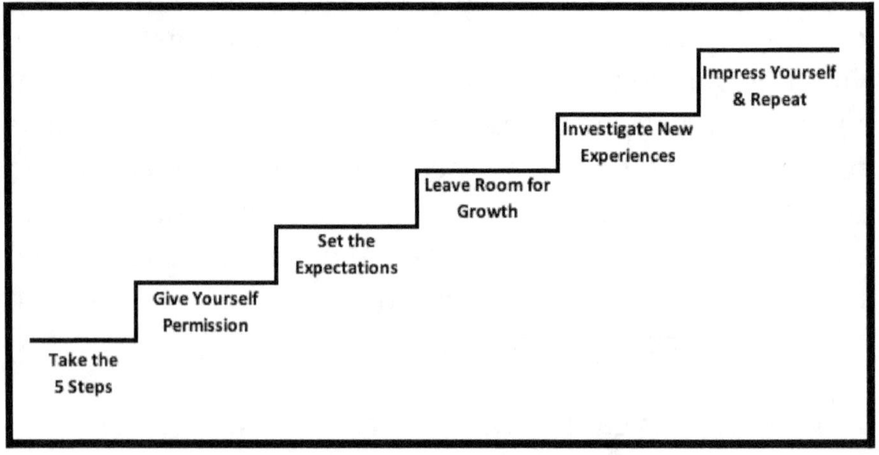

First you must make the decision to take the steps.

Step One is giving yourself permission to finally let go. Something is holding your best-self hostage. You must identify what that is. It could be a habit you know you want to break. It could be a situation you replay over and over. It could be an experience that keeps you up at night. It is thoughts that they are overly consuming. It is mentally taxing, even if subconsciously. To move forward you must give yourself permission to release it. Once you realize that time has passed and there isn't anything you can do to change it; you can finally give yourself the closure you need. I want you to always remember something, the only time something can hurt you is if you haven't accepted it. Once you have given yourself full permission to let it go, no one else can hurt you with it.

I want you to take a deep breath in. Inhale. Fill up your whole chest with air. Now repeat after me, "I have closure. I am releasing myself of ____________________________.

Now exhale. Sit for just a moment. With that exhale I want you feel your body get lighter, your mind becomes clear and the tension leave your body. Anytime you feel yourself regressing to that state of mind, repeat this exercise. Repeat as often as you need to. Permission granted.

Step Two is to set the expectation. Now that you have given yourself permission to move forward, you have to put those around you on notice. Set the expectation for them that you have let that hurt go, that habit go, and are moving forward. Give them the opportunity to help and support you by not bringing up those memories, experiences, or bringing the habits around you. If they choose not to support you, this gives you the responsibility to put yourself first. You may need to separate yourself from some people and places until you have fully stepped out of this phase. At this point, you should be the most honest with yourself. This step could be the longest to step through, and toughest to maintain. You will need to have a strong will for change. You have made it this far. Use your affirmations and mile markers to stay on track and steadfast.

Step Three is to allow yourself room to grow. In this step you start to collaborate with the supporters you have, as you are getting stronger. Think about your current status. Who is in your support system? Who in your support system looks up to you? Who is already showing you they are impressed with your progress? On days when you don't feel your strongest, you get to borrow their belief in you. You are still growing. Just like trees when they are first planted and working to embed their roots; sometimes you will need support to lean on. Through this phase you may catch yourself questioning yourself. That is okay too. You are growing and transforming. Your questions will start to be more forward thinking. This will sometimes get uncomfortable, but that is how you know you're reaching the next level.

Step Four is your investigative stage. This step has the potential to bring a lot of excitement and some moments of uncertainty. It is a mix of both because you are now exploring parts of yourself and things you've never unlocked before. Explore your interests. Find new hobbies, and things/places you enjoy. You will start to have "ah ha" moments more frequently. Can you envision what it will feel like to have complete mental and emotional freedom? This is the time to start creating new experiences, meet new people, generate new memories. How do you think this will start to change the world around you? How will it change your immediate environment? What will it look like to see and be impressed with yourself? Start thinking of things that will make you look back at your reflection everyday with pride. You are one step closer to *your* freedom.

Step Five is the culmination of all your work and coming to fruition. From this point forward you are able to walk, talk and exude the confident person you are destined to be. In this step you are able to start working on the list of ways to continue to impress yourself. This step is continuous; once you have reached this level you will never stop impressing yourself. It is your *upward* spiral and you are now allowed and have earned every right to do what impresses *you* over and over again; day after day, year after year.

The only person you are in competition with, is and will always be, the person starting back at you in the mirror. From the moment you were born the steps you've taken or haven't taken in life have led you here. No one else has ever walked the *exact* steps you have so how is it even *possible* to "compete" with them? Environment is what you create it to be. Your journey is *yours*, never forget that.

Friend! You did it! Thank you for sharing with me and allowing me to share with you. Looking at your revolutions, the sky's the limit for you. Now *that* is definitely something worth being impressed with. From this point forward, I want you to keep adding to the list. Come up with new things as often as you can. If you want, you can come back and tell me about it. Now get out there; #ImpressYourself and repeat as necessary. Just as Lao Tzu said, "The journey of a thousand miles begins with one step." Take your first step and we are glad to be on the journey with you.

#ImpressYourself

#ReflectAndDiscuss

1. What parts of the book resonated with you and/or moved you emotionally?

2. Could you relate to the concepts and feel compelled to complete the writing prompts?

3. Which chapter stood out the most to you?

4. Were there any specific lines or ideas you wrote down?

5. Would you add or take away any steps to impressing yourself?

6. What does #ImpressYourself mean to *you*?

7. If you had to describe this book to someone in 5 words, what would you say?

About the Author

Candace Thompson resides in Columbia SC and is an IT professional specializing in Training and Development. With a BA in Psychology from the University of South Carolina, she has spent over 10 years studying human behavior and self-identity. Candace is the Founder and Chief Visionary Officer of *Canvases With Candace LLC.* A mobile paint event company utilizing her expertise in technical training and psychology, to offer a "soul therapy" session for the artists. With the company tagline of "You are an artist, your life is a masterpiece," she guides the artists, and now her readers through a journey of self-discovery and relaxation. Candace is also a community speaker through her affiliation with Toastmasters International. She has been writing since childhood and previously "self-published" using construction and notebook paper.

While this is her first published book; she was impressed with herself then, but even *more* impressed with herself now.

Connect with Us

Please join our #ImpressYourselfCommunity:

    Facebook: @#ImpressYourselfCommunity

    Email: impressyourselfbook@gmail.com

    YouTube: ImpressYourselfCommunity

To connect with the author, Candace Thompson:

    Facebook: @Candacethewordartist

    Instagram: @Candacethewordartist

To connect with the artist, Canvases with Candace:

    Facebook: @CanvasesWithCandaceLLC

    Instagram: @CanvasesWithCandace

    On the Web: www.canvaseswithcandace.com

#YourThoughts

163

#ImpressYourself